Centre for
Faith and Spirituality
Loughborough University

the relationships revolution

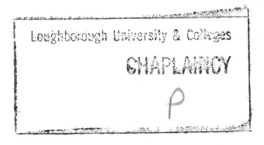

nigel d. pollock

the relationships revolution

inter-varsity press

INTER-VARSITY PRESS
38 De Montfort Street, Leicester LE1 7GP, England
© Nigel D. Pollock 1998

Unless otherwise stated, Scripture quotations in this publication are from the Holy Bible, New International Version. Copyright © 1973, 1978, 1984 by International Bible Society. Used by permission of Hodder & Stoughton Ltd. All rights reserved. 'NIV' is a registered trademark of International Bible Society. UK trademark number 1448790.

The extract on p. 12 is from 'Faith Healing' in *Whitsun Weddings* by Philip Larkin, and is reproduced by permission of the publishers, Faber and Faber Ltd.

The poem on pp. 101–102, 'I wish I was me girlfriend' by Steve Ayers, is reproduced by permission of the author.

The extract on pp. 165–166 is from 'Growing Pains' by Jamie Owens, copyright © Bud John Song/EMI Christian Music Publishing. Administered by CopyCare, PO Box 77, Hailsham BN27 3EF, UK.

First published 1998
Reprinted 1999 (twice)

British Library Cataloguing in Publication Data
A catalogue record for this book is available from the British Library.

ISBN 0-85111-583-7

Set in Gill Sans Light
Typeset by Avocet Typeset, Brill, Aylesbury, Bucks
Printed in Great Britain by The Guernsey Press Co. Ltd, Channel Islands

Inter-Varsity Press is the book-publishing division of the Universities and Colleges Christian Fellowship (formerly the Inter-Varsity Fellowship), a student movement linking Christian Unions in universities and colleges throughout Great Britain, and a member movement of the International Fellowship of Evangelical Students. For information about local and national activities write to UCCF, 38 De Montfort Street, Leicester LE1 7GP.

the relationships revolution

contents

preface

This book has grown out of the Relationships Revolution project – an ongoing initiative by the Universities and Colleges Christian Fellowship to provide positive biblical teaching and realistic, practical help in the area of sexuality and relationships. It has been produced with the help of many people. I am grateful for their honesty, seriousness and willingness to help. Students also have contributed by their openness during the Relationships Revolution meetings, which has been touching and humbling. Many have said how they wish that others could learn from their mistakes.

For myself, I have not arrived. Much of what is spoken of here comes from my own struggles and failures. Friends have stood by me and with me over the years. Their commitment to me has enabled me to continue to learn. These struggles are not over yet, nor is the battle finally won. These pages are offered by fellow travellers who know what it is to fail and are still committed to pressing on. I am more conscious than ever of our need of forgiveness and help.

I have spoken with several Christian leaders who have felt unqualified to speak and teach on this subject – through ignorance and lack of experience, or disqualified through knowledge and too much experience! But the issues are there and will not go away. We must be willing to face them with integrity. The Bible has much to say about them. If we are to see growth and change in our relationships, we must not be afraid to confront the truth, even (or perhaps especially) if that truth is painful for us personally. Writing some of this book was painful, and reading some of it may be painful for you too.

I am concerned to see people living distinctive, authentic Christian lives; enjoying relationships which do not uncritically adopt the norms of society, but which dare to be different; and experiencing friendships which rise above mediocrity and demonstrate the radical difference that Christ can make.

The need for positive biblical teaching and realistic practical help is ongoing. The challenge facing Christians is to give that help and to live out that teaching to the full.

Nigel D. Pollock

The Relationships Revolution working party
Jenny Brown, Alyson Evans, Anne Graham, Jon Hicks, Nigel Pollock, Tim Rudge, Lisa Rush, Andrew Shudall, Nikki Smith, Leila Stewart, Angela Styring, Claire Thompson

oh oh no !
no another book on!
ationships
oh no !

not another book on
relationships !

Everywhere we turn, people offer advice and guidance: how to find the perfect partner, how to be a better lover, what to do to keep love alive in a long-term relationship …

We are all searching for love. But the intimacy we crave – knowing and being known, security, and real friendship – often proves elusive. We want to trust people, but are afraid of being hurt. We want to be open with people, but find it hard to be vulnerable. We want to be committed to people, but struggle to sustain our commitment.

People let us down. We hurt those we care for most deeply. The very best experiences are difficult to reproduce. People move on, move out, grow old and die.

The thirst for intimacy is at the very centre of our being, but is not easily quenched. Yet sometimes we glimpse what could be possible. Our experience of friendship and love gives us a taste of what we could be and would like to be. When we experience the care of other people and begin to develop closeness and intimacy with them, we experience immense privileges and blessings.

the relationships revolution

What we are aiming for in this book is

- to go beyond trite and superficial advice
- to transcend romantic ideals and notions
- to have our relationships turned upside down and inside out
- to discover and learn together and to be the best that we can be.

looking looking R R for love
looking

1. looking for love

Her eyes were soft.
The moment was here.
She leaned over
and whispered in his ear:
'Do you love me?'
Thoughts raced through his mind.
Did she really *want* him?
What had he done to deserve this bounty?
Did God exist?
Who invented liquid soap and why?
'Do you love me?'
Staring into her eyes he knew
that she really needed to hear it.
But for the first time in his life
he knew that these were no longer just words.
If he said it – it would be a lie.
'Do you love me?' she whispered.
'Do you love me?'
It will not be tonight.
The answer is 'No.'

These words come from the movie *The Sure Thing*. It tells the story of a student who travels from his university on the east coast of the United States to meet with 'the sure thing' – a girl who will definitely sleep with him. In the course of his journey he discovers that sex and love are not the same thing. He had travelled across a continent but had not found the love he was looking for.

we are all looking for love

The search for love is one of the most urgent quests in life. The giving and receiving of love is one of the highest and purest expressions of our humanity. Yet this love we ache to experience often proves elusive. Loneliness is an unspoken reality for many, whether the obvious loneliness of those on the edge of the crowd, or the everyday loneliness we all experience from time to time. Few of us acknowledge that we are lonely. We put on our best party masks, but behind the façade the fear is always there: we are scared of being left out, of being denied affirmation and affection. Feeling lonely is scary. Sometimes our early experiences of love gone wrong can drive us back on our own resources; our willingness to take risks is moderated by deep hurt.

Where can we find someone who will truly love us and let us love them in return? This quest has been the central preoccupation of countless poems, songs, novels and movies. We want to reach out to those around us in a meaningful way, but this simple desire gives rise to complex emotions. We look for first love, true love, or the love of our lives, searching for the love which could make the critical difference.

In everyone there sleeps a sense of life lived according to love
To some it means the difference they could make by loving others,
But across most it sweeps as all they might have been had they
been loved.

(Philip Larkin, 'Faith Healing')

The prospect is tantalizing, but the search is not easy. The idea of love is often better than the reality. The thrill of the chase is preferable to the capture; the search for love requires risk and courage. Sometimes we are successful, and joy and excitement light up our lives. The experience of shared acceptance, affection and intimacy brings immense joy and hopes. Yet often we are taken to the threshold of lifelong commitment only for the door to slam in our face. We are rarely prepared for the rejection, disappointment and pain we encounter.

Have you ever loved anybody who has let you down?

I have never loved anyone and I do not think I ever will. I don't believe I am capable of Love. Love for me is like winning the lottery; it's just something that happens to someone else. (Sean, 19)

But despite the difficulties and hurts, we want to be loved and try to remain optimistic. Instinctively, we know what we want. We are dissatisfied with shallow relationships of mutual convenience and self-centred indifference. We keep looking and hoping. We give our objective different names – happiness, success, achievement, family, wild sex – but basically we are looking for love.

All anyone really wants to know is how to find love, and how to keep it for ever and ever, amen. We are all searching for clues to solve the biggest conundrum of all: how to be happy. It's just that the road to the palace of happiness leads through the kingdom of sexual experience; to have good sex might mean to be in love, might mean to be truly happy, the equation goes. And hope springs eternal. (*The Face*)

what is love, anyway?

What is love? It seems such an obvious question, but what would your definition be? You may struggle to find an answer. Part of the problem is the way we use language. Love can mean sentiment, as in 'Love is … never having to say you're sorry.' But this is not what you mean when you say, 'I love chocolate.' Love can mean sex, as in 'making love'; but 'I love you' murmured in the throes of passion is (one hopes) quite different from the statement 'I love my dog.' People give different values to the word. For some, saying 'I love you' is harder than divulging their PIN number. Others utter the phrase easily and frequently.

Love is not just words. There is something there – a deep mystery, profound questions, a miracle, emotions and actions – which is not easily explored.

Love has three key components:

- *need* – 'You make me feel complete.'
- *appreciation* – 'I think you are great.'
- *gift* – 'This is my present to you.'

We are all looking for significance. We want to be needed.

We are all looking for affirmation. We want to be appreciated.

We are all looking for people who will give themselves to us and receive our love. We want to be trusted and to trust.

We are looking for open, intimate relationships where we can share our deepest selves, without fear of being hurt or turned away. The problem is that we tend to look for love in the wrong place.

looking in the wrong place

Jesus once told this story:

There was a man who had two sons. The younger one said to his father, 'Father give me my share of the estate.' So he divided his property between them.

Not long after that, the younger son got together all he had, set off for a distant country and there squandered his wealth in wild living. After he had spent everything, there was a severe famine in that whole country, and he began to be in need. So he went and hired himself out to a citizen of that country, who sent him to his fields to feed pigs. He longed to fill his stomach with the pods that the pigs were eating, but no-one gave him anything.

looking for love

When he came to his senses, he said, 'How many of my father's hired men have food so spare, and here I am starving to death! I will set out and go back to my father and say to him: Father, I have sinned against heaven and you. I am no longer worthy to be called your son; make me like one of your hired men.' So he got up and went to his father.

But while he was still a long way off, his father saw him and was filled with compassion for him; he ran to his son, threw his arms around him and kissed him.

The son said to him, 'Father, I have sinned against heaven and against you. I am no longer worthy to be called your son.'

But his father said to his servants, 'Quick! Bring the best robe and put it on him. Put a ring on his finger and sandals on his feet. Bring the fattened calf and kill it. Let's have a feast and celebrate. For this son of mine was dead and is alive again; he was lost and is found.' So they began to celebrate.

Meanwhile, the older son was in the field. When he came near the house, he heard music and dancing. So he called one of the servants and asked him what was going on. 'Your brother has come,' he replied, 'and your father has killed the fattened calf because he has him back safe and sound.'

The older brother became angry and refused to go in. So his father went out and pleaded with him. But he answered his father, 'Look! All these years I've been slaving for you and never disobeyed your orders. Yet you never even gave me a young goat so I could celebrate with my friends. But when this son of yours who has squandered your property with prostitutes comes home, you kill the fattened calf for him!'

'My son,' the father said, 'you are always with me, and everything I have is yours. But we had to celebrate and be glad, because this brother of yours was dead and is alive again; he was lost and is found.' (Luke 15:11–32)

At the start of the story it becomes clear that the younger son does not love his father. He does not need his father. He wants to try things for himself, and goes off to a foreign country. He wants his share of the property now. He does not appreciate his father. In asking for his inheritance in the present, he is wishing his father was dead. He takes his money and himself away.

The father loves the son. He appreciates the son. When we see how the son later behaved, we might wonder how his father could have loved him; but the father makes him free and lets him go. It breaks his heart. It divides the family and the property. He misses the son all the time he is away. Everything the son has has come from the father. Even when he goes away he is still living on the father's gifts.

We are not told if the son finds love in the far country. He has a fortune to spend; money attracts people and can buy fun, presents and companions. The problem is this: that the son's resources are now finite. What he has will run out. He has capital, but had he stayed at home he would have had income. He has traded a relationship based on identity for a relationship based on material possessions. Who he is has become less important than what he can buy and own. Eventually, his resources are all used up.

One thing we can be sure of is that if we go looking for love on our own, we shall end up empty and lonely, frustrated and sad. We can look for love in family, sex, friends or success, and achieve some good times; but eventually our resources will run out. Our capacity to forgive, our reservoir of strength, our health and life are all finite. We know from our own experiences that families break up, beauty has a sell-by date, friends leave, success fades and people die. The son ends up in a situation where he is marginalized from society, looking after animals his own culture considered unclean. He does for a stranger menial tasks that he never had to do for his father. All his priorities are changed. His horizon has narrowed to the point that it is filled by the garbage eaten by the pigs. Even this desire is unsatisfied. 'Nobody gave him anything.' *No gift, no appreciation, no need – no love.*

There is a kind of insanity in his situation. This is what the Bible calls sin. Sin is not primarily 'naughty things', but living life running away from God. Our hearts become corrupted, our circumstances second best.

looking in the right place

What happens next is that the son comes to his senses. He does so precisely because he has been a failure in the far country. Had he been successful, he might not have realized the poverty of his circumstances; but in his heart he would still have been far away from the father who knew and loved him. For some, success gives rise to pride and an unwillingness to consider and evaluate their true situation. The son sees that he would be better off at home. He remembers that his father is a better master to his servants than the master he is now serving. He decides to return.

The son makes the mistake of wanting to be accepted back on the basis of his own activity; he hopes that his father will take him on as a hired man. Selfishness conditions us to think selfishly. It becomes ingrained in our character. The son should have realized that, having broken the relationship, he had no right to dictate the terms on which it could be restored. This is the mistake of religion. Religion imagines that we can decide the terms on which we will serve and know God. Jesus did not come to start a religion. The heart of the Christian message is seen in the picture of the father running to meet the son. In that culture, an old man running displayed a lack of dignity. The extravagant love of the father causes him to run while the son is still a long way off, to protect, restore, welcome and bless him. The father gives the son more than he had had before, and the son discovers at home all he had been looking for while he was away.

This story tells us a great deal about what God is like – a loving Father committed to reconciliation with his self-centred children. In the Bible, we see this supremely not in a story, but in a historic event. While we were still a long way off, Jesus came to do what we could not do. Jesus Christ, God himself, stretched his arms wide. On the cross, he dealt with our pain, guilt and selfishness, so that we could be welcomed back. A relationship is now possible on the Father's terms. Because Jesus rose, he is alive now. You can know *about* Marx or Muhammad or Buddha, but you can *know* Jesus for yourself, and this makes a world of difference. Only he will love you one hundred per cent as you are; only God's love is unconditional. Only God can give you the help and power to live and love and be loved. Only God can forgive you, befriend you and give you eternal life. This is the free gift he offers each one of us.

Many – Christians too – have not grasped this truth. Some still try to earn God's approval. Others try to fill the emptiness of their hearts themselves. The search for love is the search for reality. The search for reality is the search for truth. The search for truth is the search for God.

have you found love?

Do you know that God loves you? God appreciates you. He knows everything about you and you are special to him. You do not need to pretend with God. He loves you as you are. Even though you have hurt and rejected him, he yearns for you to come home. God has given his only Son for you. Forgiveness and eternal life are his free gift. His death on the cross was the greatest thing anybody has ever done or will do for you. You may know this in your head, but is it a reality for you?

Do you love God? Do you appreciate anything of his compassion, care and commitment? Do you glimpse his love and faithfulness? Do you recognize your need of God? Are you willing to hand over control of your life, or are you going to keep being your own boss, trying to work things out for yourself? Are you willing to give yourself to God wholly and completely, holding nothing back? Christians are people who have given their lives to God and are now God's friends.

This does not answer all our problems or solve all the difficulties we face, but it is the first great truth. God is love and all love comes from him. You may not believe this. You may still be looking for love in a far country. One day you may wonder if there is more, and realize it is time to come home.

There is also an older brother in the story, who has never left his

looking for love

father. The older brother has a problem too. His reaction to his brother's homecoming demonstrates a profound misunderstanding of his father's nature. He feels unappreciated, and so gives his labour grudgingly, allowing bitterness to take root. This distorted view of his father affects the way he views his younger brother. Anger keeps him away from the party. But the father loves this son too. He leaves the party to go and find him. He begs him to come in, and reasserts his love. The distortions of the elder brother's thinking are dealt with tenderly. The relationship is reinforced; the father calls him 'my son'. The appreciation is there ('you are always with me') and the reality is spelled out ('everything I have is yours'). This encounter with the father has implications for the relationship between the brothers. The older brother calls the prodigal 'this son of yours'; the father calls him 'your brother'.

Jesus tells the story of these two brothers to a mixed group of outcasts and religious leaders. The religious leaders have been complaining that Jesus is friendly with sinners. The older brother's coldness and anger mirrors the attitude of the religious leaders. Cold religiosity is not love. It is possible to be religious and know about God, without really knowing God at all. Jesus came to find the lost. Some of those nearest home can be the most lost of all.

You may have grown up in a religious home or even have had a Christian upbringing. You haven't dismissed God, but you may have developed a distorted view of his nature. There may be a veneer of respectability over your life; you may have firm views about right and wrong; you may be working hard; you may go to church or belong to a Christian group; but beneath the surface there is bitterness and frustration and no real understanding of the love of God.

A living relationship with God is not an alternative to life in its fullness. It is the foundation of a full life.

Jesus said:
'I have come that they may have life, and have it to the full.'
(John 10:10)

19

I spent years looking for love. My parents never seemed to have any time for me. I tried to make teachers like me by working hard at school. I won prizes and played in the first fifteen, but still I felt empty inside. I started going out with girls and went through a string of relationships. My mates thought I had it all – but I knew I had nothing. It was in my third year at university that I heard about Jesus. I finally found the love I had been looking for. More accurately, he came looking for me. I look back with regret on the wasted years, but I'm so glad that there weren't more. (Peter, 25)

The search for love is the most important issue in sex and relationships. My concern is not to overlook other issues, but to point you to the place where answers begin. My desire is not to produce a list of rules and regulations, but that you should come to know God's truth and healing in these areas of your life.

The good news is this: no matter who you are or what you have done, you matter a great deal to God. Jesus came to seek and save the lost. The party begins when you say 'Yes!' and decide that it's time to come home.

issues in sex & relationships

2. issues in sex and relationships

The orgasm has replaced the cross as the focus of longing and the centre of fulfilment in our society.

Malcolm Muggeridge

You don't have to be an expert to realize that our society is obsessed with sex. Our culture exploits and misrepresents sexuality in numerous ways. A distorted approach to sexuality dominates our thinking. The biggest distortion is that sex is seen as the vehicle that will deliver what our hearts long for.

what do we long for?

- *Perfection*: in a world of brokenness and pain we long for things to be so much better.
- *Intimacy*: faced with loneliness and difficulties in human relationships, we long for true love.
- *Rescue*: faced with tiredness, frustration and powerlessness, we long for something that will make the critical difference to us.

These longings of our hearts are deeply rooted in the human

condition. They point to the gap between all that we could be and all that we are. We are continually reminded of the heights of human achievement and the depths of human depravity; the same news bulletin can cover acts of heroism and crimes of unspeakable brutality. The world we live in offers various promises to make things better and deliver all we desire. These are packaged as religion, philosophy, material possessions, travel, success in the workplace, power and influence, fame and recognition, relationships, fitness, family, or any combination of these. These ideas are fuelled by advertising, peer pressure, literature and the media.

Many of us have tried them and found them to be ultimately empty. We try our best and sometimes find a little happiness, but often become cynical and refuse to be consoled by another false hope or an empty illusion. It is not that these aspirations are wrong in themselves, but the way they are presented often leads us to believe that they will make the critical difference to us. In our society, many people believe this of sex and relationships especially. But whenever anything becomes a central focus, we must be willing to evaluate what it offers and question whether it is able to deliver.

what does sex promise?

- *Perfection*: it's got to be perfect, a sublime moment, one experience that will transport you.
- *Intimacy*: sex promises closeness, to know and be known; it offers the key to intimacy.
- *Rescue*: a way out of loneliness, an escape from ugliness.

Someone will give you something that will rescue you, lifting you above your anxieties and fears.

These components combine in different fantasies. The *sexual fantasy* tends to revolve around physical perfection; the one with the perfect body and most beautiful face will be the best lover. Someone who looks good will be good, and with that person we will experience true intimacy. If we could find such a person, our lives would be complete; we would experience great sex, find true love and receive all we hope and long for. In some scenarios the fantasy takes the initiative, but in most cases, all that is offered is a willing and compliant partner to fulfil our every sexual whim. Expertly packaged, the imagery can be intoxicating, and even looking at images of the perfect body can transport us briefly beyond our everyday lives.

The *romantic fantasy* centres upon an ideal character. The perfect person has status, dresses immaculately, is caring and compassionate, lives in a house beside the ocean, cooks superbly, and is always kind, willing to listen and available. Such a person would be thoughtful and spontaneous, get on with your mother and like children and animals. He or she would be faithful, accepting of who you are, and capable of great passion and commitment. This fantasy usually culminates not in orgasm, but in riding off into the sunset to begin filling the house by the ocean with children and designer furniture. Encountering such characters in fiction can offer us a momentary respite from the mundane.

It would be easy to stereotype these fantasies, the first as male and the second as female. The reality, I suspect, is more complex. Both men and women have sexual and romantic fantasies. They lead us to behave in different ways in different situations: in a night-club we may pursue our sexual fantasies; in our relationships our romantic ones. Such unacknowledged fantasies can be destructive, especially when the boundaries between fantasy and reality become blurred.

The problem with these packages is that they offer false hope and create unrealistic expectations. The tyranny of perfection can leave us frustrated by every real person we encounter. We find ourselves trying to relate to other people who are flawed and imperfect, just as we are. True intimacy has to start from this realistic basis. Other people are not there to satisfy our needs and desires. Part of growing up is beginning to realize our responsibilities to give to other people rather than being preoccupied with what we can get. Yet the sexual fantasy continues to be compelling, and many see it as their best hope of rescue.

does sex deliver what it promises?
perfection

Sex can be great. At its best it can be one of the few experiences that transport us above ourselves, enabling us to be selfless – to give and receive exquisite pleasure and to celebrate being alive. Our experiences may often be more ordinary than that, but still pleasurable, weaving a thread of commitment and enjoyment through our lives and relationships.

But this is clearly not the experience of many. Were it so easy, there would be no demand for the glut of advice which the media market. Our experiences seem one-dimensional and less than perfect. Glimpsing perfection can leave us all the more frustrated.

Even when things are going well, 'always and for ever' are such elusive qualities. There is a crisis in commitment in our culture. Marriages do not last, and other commitments fare even worse. The average length of time partners live together, outside marriage is three years. People don't stay together, because the perfection they long for is difficult to find, and what they do find is hard to keep. Even great sex does not keep people together.

intimacy

We seem to find physical intimacy the easiest kind to achieve. But physical intimacy does not necessarily lead to emotional intimacy. Some people go looking for sex without strings attached; some find it easier to have sex than to say 'I love you'. The more you have physical intimacy with different partners, the easier it is to become hardened to emotional intimacy. We cannot kiss and talk at the same time. Most people realize that sex does not equal love.

Everybody in the office thought Angela was absolutely gorgeous. She was living with her boyfriend. One day in a conversation she revealed that every morning she set her alarm for five o'clock so that she could put on her make-up before her boyfriend woke up. She didn't want him to see her without her make-up on. She was physically intimate with him, but was not known and accepted for who she was.

Sex does not deliver intimacy. It may help intimacy, but is not the key to it.

rescue

Sex can make you feel better for a while, but does it really change you? It can change your relationships for better or for worse, but does it change the person you are? Does sex make you less selfish, more loving, self-controlled, patient and secure, or more able to keep your promises?

Does sex really deliver what it promises? You must decide if sex can make the critical difference to you.

who can deliver the goods?

Can anything or anyone deliver the perfection, intimacy and rescue we crave? What are the alternatives?

Ourselves. But how do we cope with insecurities and anxieties, weaknesses and experiences? Can we really find perfection, intimacy and rescue in our own strength?

The experts. There are many who are willing to offer advice. They are doing their best, but they are limited. They are engaging with complex issues, and they are all living life for the first time just as we are. They may have helpful insights, but they cannot give us the resources to cope with life's challenges.

A lover. It is tremendous to know intimacy and acceptance. But even if you find those things in somebody – even if you find something really close to what you are looking for – will it last? Can it last? Can one person carry the burden of all your hopes and desires? All too often, those we love the most hurt us most. Rejection and hurt give way to cynicism and throw us back to the first option: working it out for ourselves.

I meet many people trying to cope with difficult situations but not knowing where to turn for help:

- scared that they don't know the questions, let alone the answers
- physically mature, but emotionally uncertain

- struggling with their sexual identity
- trying to cope with guilt about thoughts and actions in the past and present
- addicted to masturbation and fantasy
- hurting from being messed around in a relationship
- in pain from sexual abuse, their silent screams perhaps unknown to anyone
- longing for a relationship after years of nothing

We all need help. Not trite answers or secondhand opinions, but realistic, practical help. In my own battles, what has helped most is compassion and commitment. You can guarantee that, whatever you are struggling with, others have faced it before and still face it today.

what do you struggle with?

The Relationships Revolution group has done a number of surveys with Christian students, exploring the issue of sex and relationships. The results have been consistent over a number of years. The majority have never heard any Christian teaching on relationships or sex-related matters. Seventy per cent feel there is no-one they would feel free to talk to about personal relationships and sexuality. Of those who do talk, most would go to a friend their own age, rather than to an older person, parent, health professional or minister. This often leads to a sharing of ignorance rather than to any positive progress.

Our surveys identified the main pressure points for Christian young people in the sexual realm as

- peer pressure to be sexually active (30%)
- not having a boyfriend/girlfriend (25%)
- petting; how far is it OK to go in a relationship? (22%)
- sexual guilt (18%)
- controlling thought life (15%)

When these people are asked what they struggle with personally, there has been very little change in the ranking over six years:

The men's top five
1. Masturbation
2. Images on film, video and magazines
3. The way women dress
4. Memories of the past
5. Not having a girlfriend

The women's top five
1. Fear of singleness
2. Not having a boyfriend
3. Memories of the past
4. Pressure from boyfriend
5. Masturbation

Significant numbers also struggle with homosexual feelings, with living in mixed accommodation, and with the temptation to go out with somebody who is not a Christian.

The very idea of taking a stand on some of these issues is under threat. Although some will respect those who do so, others will interpret such a stand as an indictment of their own practices. Many people adopt a belief system which enables them to justify their past and present practices. The true cost of sexual misadventure is rarely contemplated in the media because people have learned to make sense of their own experience and insecurities by means of careful adjustments to their values and conscience. It is deemed a good thing to make mistakes and learn from them as a passport to security and satisfaction. A lot of young people are either influenced by this kind of model or have begun to adopt it for themselves. From the TV presenter who says, 'If I had not slept with three men before I got married I would never have been able to enjoy sex with my husband', via the teenager who thinks, 'Unless I get some experience I'll never be able to be happy', it is a small step for Christian young people to start thinking, 'God can help me learn from my experiences, so why not go ahead?' This experimental approach to sexuality not only disregards God's law; it dismisses the depth of hurt and the serious consequences which accompany it. Sexual guilt is a huge issue among young people, and Christians are certainly not exempt.

> I would really like a boyfriend. I feel pretty left out a lot of the time and wonder whether anyone will ever love me or find me attractive. I long to be close to someone and am worried I'll be left on the shelf. Singleness really scares me; I'd love to get married and have a family. There's a guy on my course I quite fancy. He isn't a Christian but maybe I should think about him (Sarah, 21)

> I sometimes wonder why God made me a woman at all. Why not an amoeba with no worries on the issue of sex – finding a partner, wondering if this seemingly mythical man actually exists? I know male–female relationships are not always what they are cracked up to be, and many of my friends are divorced or separated, but does that mean that I should be denied the chance of finding out for myself what intimacy with a man could truly be, within God's love? Isn't there one man in the whole world for me? And another thing: is the problem that I am so ugly and sinful that God decided I should remain terminally celibate? (Mary, 32)

> My main struggle is with masturbation. I just find that I always seem to be thinking about sex. All kinds of images fill my mind and I am constantly fantasizing, imagining people naked or making love. Masturbation seems to be the only way I can control myself. (John, 19)

How would you respond to these people? What advice would you give? Answers don't come easily. We live in a landscape without markers, a moral wasteland where there is no shared moral code and few features to navigate by. We try our best, but we do not know what to do.

What do you personally struggle with the most?

Where are you looking for love?

Can anything help us navigate the wasteland?

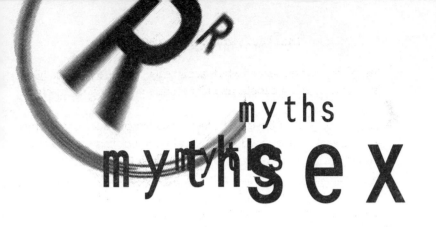

3. myths about sex

The great enemy of the truth is very often not the lie: deliberate, contrived and dishonest; but the myth: persistent, persuasive and unrealistic.

John F. Kennedy

Sex is the most talked about and most thought about subject in contemporary western society. Alt.sex is currently Usenet's busiest newsgroup. It is read by 450,000 people worldwide, even though only about 70% of the Usenet sites carry the group. By the age of eighteen the average person will have watched nine thousand actual or suggested acts of sexual intercourse on television. I have no idea how they work these things out, but I can easily believe it.

Society's views on what is appropriate continue to shift. When I was a teenager, if there was a topless scene on television, the boys at school would be talking about it the next day. If you had not seen the programme in question you were acutely disappointed because you knew that another opportunity was not likely to arise for some time. Now, there are so many more sexually explicit scenes. Images that fuelled the adolescent fantasies of my generation now feature in

29

adverts, as well as movies, almost on a daily basis. Any newsagent's shop presents us with an array of headlines promising to help you 'find a partner', 'enjoy bigger and better orgasms', 'experience the ultimate position'. People are desperate for advice on how to find and keep meaningful relationships.

A new group of experts has arisen to try to cope with this need. Agony aunts and uncles give popular advice in newspapers and magazines. 'Incredibly, 24% of girls would consult a magazine problem page for advice on sexual matters. That beats asking Dad, a sister/brother, boyfriend, teacher or family planning clinic' (*Sunday Mirror*/Family Planning Association). Television chat shows and discussion programmes explore issues of commitment, fulfilment and satisfaction. Some American colleges employ love coaches to give advice and help on all aspects of relationships.

The legacy of all this is that everyone is supposed to know everything about sex. We have a greater access to information than ever before. Sexual activity is an expected part of social interaction, before and outside long-term relationships.

I am glad that some of the taboos of a previous generation have been dispensed with. Many were not healthy and led to hypocrisy or oppressive legalism. List of rules without understanding became increasingly meaningless. But it is tragic that this new freedom of information and behaviour has produced such a slanted, one-sided view which has in fact given little help and promoted little choice. The liberal society can be the least tolerant of all – you are free as long as you exercise your freedom in the way expected of you.

It may well be better to have technical information about sex than the ignorance of previous generations. Educators, columnists and parents do their best to cover the basics of technique, health and safety, but people's own experience inevitably shapes their opinions about sex. This is often unacknowledged, and the advice of 'experts' may simply validate personal choices made in the past. We often lack humility in addressing the big questions that are harder to understand. We do not know everything. We are incredibly complex beings, and relating together as men and women is a complicated business. We may well get caught in the crossfire between opinion and experience that passes for truth in society.

There is a growing body of values and ideas on what is right and wrong or acceptable in the area of sexuality. The basis of this morality, or the assumptions upon which these value judgments are based, is often difficult to discern. People frequently try to suggest that issues of sexuality and relationships can be handled without reference to biblical morality.

The morality by which most people live is not absolute. It is not to be imposed on other people. The ideas that shape our choices, expectations and lifestyle are more often rooted in popular mythology than in truth. It is worth examining some of these persistent, persuasive and unrealistic myths which have become part of the fabric of western society.

'sex is the most important thing in life'

Sex has become a basic human right. You have the right to express your sexuality in whatever way you see fit. If you are not having sex, there is something wrong with you.

A vicar interviewed on a TV chat show said, 'If I interviewed someone who was twenty-five and still a virgin, I would think that there was something seriously wrong with them and would relate to them and counsel them on that basis.'

Sex is perceived as the key to intimacy. You do not really know somebody until you have been to bed with him or her. Yet many early encounters often take place in far from ideal circumstances, outside a context of ongoing love and commitment. One university safe-sex leaflet concluded: 'Enough of this moralizing. Sleep with whoever you want, whenever you want, but do it carefully.'

The big problem with this myth is the lack of consistency. Teenage magazines send out mixed messages. Articles on 'How to do it', with pictures of people having fun, are followed a few pages later with letters saying, 'We tried it, and we're hurting, and we need help.'

Sex is not the most important thing in life. Sexual closeness is relatively easy to achieve, but it is not the key to emotional or spiritual intimacy. Even in marriage, the idea that says 'Get the sex bit right and rest will fall into place' is the reverse of the truth.

If you did believe that sex was the most important thing in life, we would not handle it the way our society does. Anything of high value is protected, guarded and cherished. Those who reduce sex education to questions of health and safety take a minimalist view. People are more than bodies. We are minds and spirits and beings who feel. Sex and sexuality involve more than the interaction of bodies. They involve the interaction of people. You cannot put a condom on your heart or on your mind. Many people struggle with memories from the past. Others continue to feel linked with a previous partner long after the relationship has ended. Still more try to cope with a view of themselves and other people induced by sexual guilt.

'experience is a good thing'

Sexual experience with a number of different partners is a positive thing. It is important to test your sexual compatibility. This is a crucial part of building commitment. You wouldn't buy a house without checking the plumbing; 'taste and try before you buy'.

Sex has become western society's initiation right. The message that comes across clearly is that everybody is doing it. 'Start using it as soon as you are 16. By 24 you will be too old' (British Rail young person's railcard ad, featuring American sex expert Dr Ruth). Sexual experience gives you status amongst your peers and confirms your standing as an adult. If you are not sexually active, you are missing out; you are not part of the in group. You do not understand what is going on.

I'm 14 and my boyfriend is 19. I'm useless in bed as I haven't had much experience. He's had lots of girlfriends and I'm worried he compares me with them. I'd really like to please him. Can you give me some clues about how I can improve? (*Cosmopolitan*, November 1996)

The problem with this myth is that it tends to separate the physical act of intercourse from commitment and intimacy. In some cultures it is even seen as desirable for a young man to lose his virginity with the maid or a prostitute. Those who instinctively want to link sex and love would be appalled at this. But many early experiences of sex do not take place in the context of love. There is often insecurity, anxiety and a lack of mutual consideration. We can be taught from our earliest encounters that sex is about selfishness, getting what you are looking for, and achieving what you want. First experiences of anything often set the tone for the way we think about, enjoy and use it later. Sex is no different. Many people get hurt, experiencing the 'paper cup' syndrome: they feel taken up, used up, screwed up and thrown away.

Innocence is a precious thing. Virginity is something to be given away, not lost or taken.

Experience with different partners, far from enhancing commitment, often leads to the tyranny of comparison. Increasingly, we can be left searching for a composite ideal instead of appreciating a real individual.

Even in this age of safe-sex education, there is a considerable cost to sexual experience. More than 8 in every 1000 girls under the age of sixteen became pregnant in England and Wales in 1994. Over 50% of these ended in abortion. There is research that suggests a link between multiple sexual partners and infertility in later life, and between early intercourse and infertility.

'you've got to follow your feelings'

You must be true to yourself. Personal feelings are the supreme arbiter of appropriate behaviour. The question 'Is this right or wrong?' is redundant. Morality has been superseded by reality. Whatever feels good is acceptable and appropriate. Others have no right to question the decision you have made, because they cannot enter into your reality. They do not understand the force with which you feel something. Morality is a question of personal opinion. 'I did it my way – how did I know it was the right way? Because it was my way and it felt right.'

The search for happiness has become the central preoccupation of our time. Following our feelings, however, does not always deliver the result we intended. Moreover, following our feelings can leave other people scattered and damaged in our wake. We are not victims of circumstance. We have the capacity to choose, to go beyond our feelings, and to evaluate the rightness of a course of action. What is presented as being true to yourself often translates as simply pleasing yourself.

Relationships are hard work. There are times when commitment takes guts, when we are required to give far more than we receive. Some marriages get into difficulty when the first child is born. Suddenly there is someone in the household who is more selfish than you are, and the marriage crumbles as the coalition of self-serving which was its foundation comes under attack. Such situations need to be worked through rather than avoided, and that process can lead to far greater satisfaction and security.

Our feelings change over time, and are affected by our emotions, circumstances and physical condition. This fluctuation makes it difficult to assess what our true feelings are. Our feelings will also be influenced by our choices and actions. Every day we choose to do things that we may not particularly feel like doing. We also choose not to do some things that we do feel like doing. This is not a betrayal of ourselves; rather, it is necessary for our well-being, and for relationships to function properly.

If, in the quest for happiness, we simply follow our feelings, we condemn ourselves to a futile search. This is especially true in relationships where two people can have feelings at the same moment which would lead them in opposite directions.

'romantic relationships are personal and private'

As long as what you do does not hurt anybody else, no-one has the right to question how you behave within a relationship. The couple has become the basic building-block of social life, and it is an unwritten rule that couples should be left to their own devices. When two people are romantically involved, a third person is one too many.

Relationships are seen to develop in quality as they become more exclusive. Couples often make significant decisions about their lives and future without reference to anyone else. The ideal is portrayed as having all your physical, emotional and spiritual needs met by one person. Consequently, when a meaningful romantic relationship develops, long-term friends are abandoned in favour of spending time with each other.

It cannot be left to individuals to determine what is right and wrong. Actions between people always have knock-on effects, which necessarily impact all our relationships and friendships. It is difficult for a couple ever to be certain that what they are doing is not damaging or hurting other people. One of the benefits of living in society, rather than being marooned on a desert island, is that we can learn from other people. We do not make moral choices in a vacuum, but in the context of responsibility and accountability to others. Most countries have laws on issues such as the age of consent, the legitimacy of sexual relationships between family members, appropriate sexual behaviour and what is permissible in the public domain and media. Most acknowledge that some restrictions on behaviour are a good thing. 'The law concerning under-age sex is not there to spoil your fun but to protect you from all kinds of damage' (*Marie Claire*, May 1997).

It is also folly to believe that all our needs can or should be met in one relationship. Romantic relationships are stronger when conducted in the context of community and family. It is not just that our bad behaviour affects other people; their good behaviour impacts us positively. We benefit from advice, support, care, help and friendship. It is unrealistic to expect one person to fulfil the role of homemaker, provider, protector, confidante, best friend, role model for the children, handyman, spiritual mentor, career advisor, financial planner and counsellor.

If we live with open hearts and open hands we shall receive much more than if we bolt the door and try to construct our own private utopia. The best friendships and relationships are inclusive.

'romantic love is the route to happiness and freedom'

Only romantic love can deliver us from the drudgery of life. Without romance, life is monochrome.

'Someday my prince will come' is the theme tune of many lives. Hours are spent looking for Mr Right, Miss Available, Mr Presentable, Miss Adequate, Mr Right Now or Miss Anybody. Weddings are still the focus of celebration and gift-giving. Some people wait for love so anxiously that they cannot get on with the rest of their lives. Lonely hearts columns feature in broadsheet and tabloid newspapers alike. People escape into novels, soaps and movies, experiencing their hopes at second hand. Others chase the shadows of what they yearn for, leafing through magazines, chatting on sex lines, or browsing the internet. Although the shadows are insubstantial, so strong is the desire for this one transforming relationship that the counterfeits quickly become addictive.

While we wait and search, we often neglect or devalue existing friendships. Focusing so strongly on the one object we do not have blurs the many other valuable aspects of your life. Focusing on the people and opportunities around us can put the missing elements in perspective.

These myths overlap and interrelate. Together they conspire to produce a set of values which dominate our approach to sex and sexuality.

idea

4. getting the wrong idea

It was a beautiful, starry night. The perfect end to the perfect evening. James was driving Sally home after the school dance. Their route took them past a well-known parking spot. James pulled over and turned hopefully to Sally.

'Do you want to get in the back?' he asked.

'No,' she replied. 'I want to stay in the front with you.'

It is easy for us to misread the signals and pick up the wrong ideas.

The example is trivial, but there are some areas of serious confusion which can distort our thinking, influence our actions and affect our relationships.

confusion about sex

'sexuality = sex'

The biggest mistake concerning sex is to reduce all matters of sexuality to sexual activity. Sexuality is a concept that has been robbed of much of its richness. Our sexuality is far more than our capacity to have sex.

Sexuality is an important aspect of our humanity. As human beings, we are made in God's image with the ability to relate to others and to experience intimacy with them. This capacity for intimate relationship is at the heart of our sexuality. Sexuality also has to do with our identity as men and women and with being bodily creatures. The capacity for sexual intercourse is part of our sexuality, but is far from being the totality of it. Our sexuality is expressed in many different ways. It involves caring, giving, experiencing sensual pleasure, creativity, receiving and giving affection, and communicating.

Properly understood, sexuality is not something to be denied, but a part of our identity that we can enjoy. Our thirst for intimacy and our need and desire for relationships are central to our humanity. Our sexuality is part of this. We derive our sexuality from our humanity, not the other way round. The higher sex features on our agenda, the more we distort our sexuality and diminish our humanity. We are more than physical beings; sex is not just a physical act, and our sexuality is not expressed in sexual activity alone.

'sex = penetration – or not'

A second misconception concerns what constitutes sex and when sex begins. Some would define sex as penetration; sex takes place only when the penis enters the vagina, and this is what constitutes sex. 'I'm a technical virgin. I've never gone all the way, but I keep my man happy.' This is quite a minimalist definition of sex.

Increasing numbers of people, writing from different perspectives, are arguing that you can have a perfectly satisfying sex life without penetration. Those concerned to promote safe sex also contend that a safer and equally satisfying sex life can be achieved without penetrative sex being on the menu of what a couple share and enjoy. Writers from a homosexual or lesbian background argue in a similar vein. Many same-sex couples feel they can enjoy a full and satisfying sex life without penetration taking place. Some feminists advance the case that some men are far too genitally focused in their love-making, and argue that more loving relationships can be achieved without penetration. None of these people is saying that what the couple are sharing is not sex. Others believe that a couple can do anything and, as long as it stops short of penetration, it is not sex.

38

getting the wrong idea

There are various definitions of sex and where it begins. Some of these may have greater integrity than others. People preoccupied with technical virginity may have something to learn from the homosexual and feminist viewpoints mentioned above. To imagine that nakedness, mutual masturbation and orgasm can somehow be excluded from the definition of sex is dangerously short-sighted.

'you have to live with your mistakes'

A third common misconception is that sexual mistakes cannot be forgiven; that failures or misdemeanours in this area have to be lived with for the rest of your life. Many carry burdens of guilt and shame for actions they have performed or that have been done to them. The consequences of these can be profound and the memories extremely vivid; the power of the past to shape and control the way we think about ourselves and other people can be oppressive. The misuse and abuse of sex in our society have left many damaged.

The Bible does not flinch from recognizing the full horror of the human condition. One philosopher looked at the world many centuries ago and wrote:

> What is twisted cannot be straightened;
> what is lacking cannot be counted.
>
> (Ecclesiastes 1:15)

What is 'lacking' is the love that was not shown, the encouragement that was not given, the care withheld, the words not spoken. These are symptoms of a wider lack of generosity, equality, justice, hope and peace. The shortage of these things in the world cannot be measured; what is lacking in our own lives cannot be counted. What is 'twisted' are characteristics such as the desire to please ourselves, to lie, to self-destruct and to spoil. Our tendency to push others down, to ignore their need, to struggle to express affection and love – this twistedness runs through the human condition and, despite all the efforts of religion, education and politics, it is basically unchanged.

This is not an optimistic view; but we have to consider whether the diagnosis might not be current. Even recently, we have seen huge leaps in technological progress, but not much moral progress. The world is still full of poverty, and riddled with dissension, bigotry and wars. The hope that the Bible points to is not hope in religion or in human effort. It centres on the death and resurrection of Jesus. God did not sit back and hope things would get better; he intervened by sending his Son. This is what makes forgiveness possible. Sexual sin is part of a wider problem; sin as a whole. Jesus died on the cross to deal with this issue. No matter how much we have messed up, forgiveness is possible.

confusion about marriage

Some people see marriage as being just a piece of paper. A private or oral commitment is perceived to be as valid as a public declaration. They may have seen or experienced the impact of divorce at first hand.

It is true that what gives a relationship value is not going through a ceremony, but the quality of love which exists between the couple. There are people who have conducted long and successful relationships, having lived together, raised children together and grown old together without going through a marriage ceremony. There are others who go through a succession of marriages and divorces. Some regard commitment as valuable, but see marriage as hypocritical.

Others, far from being cynical, are romantically idealistic about marriage. They see marriage as the end of all their struggles and problems – the event that will enable them to live happily ever after. 'Love and marriage go together like a horse and carriage.' The white wedding with all the trimmings promises the fairytale ending. The couple sail off to live for ever under a cloudless sky, without arguments, struggles or loneliness, and with free and safe sex constantly on tap.

This may sound like a caricature, but for some the romantic ideal runs deep. One guy took me to task for saying that even Christians might continue to experience troubles and temptations once they were married. Did I not realize that when you got married, God sanctified your sexual desire so that you had thoughts only for your partner, and that he protected your relationship so that no harm would come to you? He was certain that this would be the case for him. Having suggested otherwise, I was a poor example of both faith and marriage.

Most people long for commitment in a relationship. Some see marriage as an obstacle to this, whereas for others it is the answer. What is clear is that there is a crisis in commitment across the spectrum, with neither marriages nor relationships lasting very long.

confusion about morality

People have very different ideas about what is right and wrong. We have already noticed that for some the very question is redundant. Practically everyone, however, adopts a code of conduct – some specific standards and behaviours. This is clear both from our ability to pass judgment on other people and from the prodding of our own consciences.

What is the basis for morality? On what grounds do people decide how they are going to behave? Some operate a pick-and-mix policy. They take bits and pieces they find attractive from different religious or philosophical traditions or writers, and construct their own personal code. Others adopt a comparative standard or morality, measuring themselves against other people and feeling that they are doing better or worse. Others simply try to assess the consequences of any proposed action and believe you should try to get away with as much as you can.

Does an absolute standard exist? Is there such a thing as truth which stands and goes beyond opinion, comparison and consequence? Many are attracted by that kind of certainty, but would find its implications difficult. It is not easy living without truth. The absence of an authoritative voice gives rise to moral anarchy. As G. K. Chesterton observed, when you stop believing the truth, you do not believe nothing; you believe anything. If you do not know what you stand for, you will end up falling for anything and everything. And people do.

Because anarchy is not a state we are comfortable with, we develop our own standards and try to live by them as best we can. This desire to manage our own affairs is not an easy option. Some try to cope by handing over responsibility to another: maybe they live at home and still abide by their parents' norms; or maybe they throw themselves into a work situation where the pace leaves little time for reflection. Others look for help from a guru, an 'expert' or the media. One young adult laughed, 'I'm from the TV generation. I learned life from *Brookside* and Oprah Winfrey.' Some seek refuge in religious fundamentalism, where clear-cut answers are provided without the necessity to think things through for themselves. Others learn alone. I was talking to a friend about this in his flat. He was adamant: 'I could never trust someone else to run my life.' I looked around the room. Dirty dishes were on the floor. Crumpled washing lay where it fell. Unanswered correspondence bulged on the mantelpiece. Final demands piled up on the table. He was clearly doing a good job of running himself!

What you believe may not be true. How you behave may need to change. This has to be possible for me and for you. We must be willing to explore alternatives if we are not to be misled and confused. We need to be open to considering whether the values and ideas we hold most dear are influenced by myths and misconceptions. If we are not willing to subject them to scrutiny, we inevitably close our minds to the possibility of finding greater truth.

5. knowing the truth

I am the kind of person who refers to the manufacturer's instructions as a last resort. I am far happier experimenting, making mistakes, finding things out as I go. Only when I come across a problem I cannot solve do I reluctantly drag out the instructions. They are not always easy to understand, in which case it is necessary to get in touch with the company. The manufacturers understand the product better than the user or the supplier, because they put it together. They designed it, made it and supplied it; they understand how it works and how it should function. The problem is often quite easy to solve.

It would be great if all the difficult issues we face were so easily solved. But there is no instruction booklet for life. You can get books that reveal the wisdom of the ages – like how long it takes to cook a casserole, how to get ink stains off your clothes, how to make friends and influence people, or how to be a successful manager. Plenty of people offer advice and insights, but you cannot pick up a handbook that will solve every problem that confronts us. There is no appendix listing sources of help when you are feeling lonely, asking why life does not work out the way you hoped, wondering how to find the power to change, struggling with unemployment, bereavement or promotion, choosing a course or a house, looking for a really good time on holiday, or searching how to become the person you want to be. There are books addressing each of these issues, but we try to fix one problem only to discover that something else is broken. This piecemeal approach leaves us dissatisfied. The number and complexities of the issues demand a more comprehensive solution.

The absence of a detailed handbook does not mean that we cannot consult our Maker, nor that the Maker has given us no book at all. The Bible claims to be the unique revelation of the God who made the galaxies, who created human beings in his image, and who sustains the universe by his power. The Bible's remarkable opening statement, 'In the beginning God created ...' is neither a historical observation (there were no humans present!) nor a scientific theory. The event is recorded as a fact, with the cause and effect clearly affirmed, but it is not described in the language of modern cosmology. The writer simply states the first great truth of the universe – that in the beginning was God. Before anything else existed, God was, and God created everything. He brought the cosmos into being. There was, then, something there in the beginning. That something was a someone; that someone was God; and that God is the one who has revealed himself through the Bible.

The Bible tells how the God of the universe revealed himself to the men and women he had created in his image – how he made and kept a solemn promise to create a community of people who would love and serve him together for all time. The Bible is far more than a manufacturer's manual for life. Rather, it reveals the Maker to us. It gives insights into his character, the ways in which he works, and his dealings with people throughout generations – his plans and purposes for the world he has made. God does not want us to function as his pets or as his programmed robots, but to learn to live and love freely. He is a God who is for us and with us, who is committed to people, and who wants us to grow in our love and understanding of him.

The Bible is, quite simply, the most remarkable book ever written. It alone speaks with authority on the character and purposes of

Almighty God. This is the compass that God has given us to navigate the wasteland. It is a library of sixty-six books recording God's dealings with humanity over four thousand years. This amazing treasury of different kinds of literature has many great truths to teach us.

There is much misunderstanding of the Bible and prejudice against it. The challenge is to read it for ourselves. Because it can seem daunting, it helps if we can first grasp its basic structure. We can approach it as a drama serial with four main episodes.

episode 1: God creates

In the beginning there was no death, no anxiety, no sadness, no shame. God looked at the world he had made and saw that it was good.

The pinnacle of this creation was humanity. 'The LORD God formed the man from the dust of the ground and breathed into his nostrils the breath of life, and the man became a living being' (Genesis 2:7). God made people with his own hands and brought them to life with his own breath. The direct involvement and intimacy of this picture are very moving. God made us, and he made us with a purpose. The beginning of the book of Genesis outlines this purpose.

made to be God's friends

> So God created man
>   in his own image,
> In the image of God
>   he created him;
> Male and female
>   he created them.

(Genesis 1:27)

Central to being made in God's image is a very high view of the quality of the relationship he intended us to have with him. God did a remarkable thing in choosing to make us like himself. This is the crucial factor marking out the nature of human beings from the rest of creation. All things were made by God and for God, but we, supremely, have the capacity to appreciate and respond to him. It is difficult to have a meaningful relationship with a goldfish. You can feed it and talk to it, and with a bit of imagination you could even take it for walks. But it can't talk to you or understand you or know you. You can have a different kind of relationship with someone who is like you. God made us like him so that we could relate to him in an easy and natural manner – to be his friends. This theme of friendship with God is described and developed throughout the Old and New Testaments.

made to relate to each other

The LORD God said, 'It is not good for the man to be alone. I will make a helper suitable for him' (Genesis 2:18). Just as God himself is community – Father, Son and Holy Spirit – so we, in his image, were made to be in community, to have relationships of intimacy with those who were made like us. This is why solitary confinement is still considered to be one of the worst punishments that can be inflicted on people. We thrive when we are with other people. We were made this way. Adam had a relationship with God, but God provided other people so that humanity could experience human relationships. Relationships of love and equality with other created beings were central in God's creative purposes for us.

given work to do

'God blessed them and said to them, "Be fruitful and increase in number; fill the earth and subdue it"' (Genesis 1:28a); 'The LORD God took the man and put him in the Garden of Eden to work it and take care of it' (Genesis 2:15). Adam and Eve were to look after the land and to name the animals, continuing the work God had started. Joining with God in the creative process, they were given power and dominion over the earth. There was no distinction between 'secular' and 'spiritual' work. This command to produce and reproduce is a mandate for the whole of life, a satisfying job with unlimited scope for development.

given responsibility

'The LORD God commanded man, "You are free to eat from any tree in the garden; but you must not eat from the tree of knowledge of good and evil, for when you eat of it you will surely die"' (Genesis 2:16–17). People are not God. We were made to live *for* God – so that we could enjoy him and he us. The only limit to this remarkable relationship arose from God's integrity and the nature of those he had created. The tree in the garden was not a test. It was a visible reminder that God is God. Humans are not eternal; God sustains them. Humankind is not all powerful; it is God who makes the sun shine, the seed grow, and their hearts beat. Humankind is not everywhere; it is God who oversees the ocean depths, the highest peak, the coldest planet and the furthest star. Humankind does not know everything; millennia later, powerful telescopes and microscopes continue to reveal new and uncharted territory.

Humankind was created to enjoy a living relationship with the God of the universe. This privilege is the basis for all our responsibilities. We were made to be responsible to our Creator, and responsible for the people around us and for our environment. All this was good. In the beginning our relationship with God and each other, our fulfilment in work and our handling of responsibility were all good. There were no problems in any of these areas.

episode 2: sin enters

But people turned their backs on God. We chose not to live with our responsibility. Adam and Eve disobeyed God. This had profound consequences for them, and for us. They are summarized in God's conversation with their son Cain. Cain neglected God and then killed his brother. Inevitably God had to punish him. Cain responded: 'My punishment is more than I can bear. Today you are driving me from the land, and I will be hidden from your presence; I will be a restless wanderer on the earth, and whoever finds me will kill me' (Genesis 4:13–14).

We saw that the first element in God's purpose for us at creation was that we should be his friends. Cain said, 'I will be hidden from your presence.' Relationship with God is broken. The second element was to relate easily to other people. Cain said, 'Whoever finds me will kill me.' The third element was the task of looking after the land. Cain said, 'Today you are driving me from the land.' The fourth element was responsibility. Cain had already denied this in his question, 'Am I my brother's keeper?' (verse 9). The rejection of responsibility in relationship with God has profound consequences in social relationships. As far back as Genesis 4 we see humankind alienated from God, struggling in relationships with other people, and lacking a sense of purpose and direction in life. The plight of modern women and men was summarized thousands of years ago. If Cain's statement does not tug at your heartstrings, you have not understood what it is about.

To this day, the consequences of this severed relationship with God affect us deeply. The breaking of this crucial relationship at the pinnacle of creation causes everything else to be fractured. Not only are God's creative purposes for humankind broken, but our very capacity to achieve that purpose has been damaged. We are unable to achieve intimacy with God. We are unable to enjoy intimacy with other people. The relationship between the sexes is distorted and corrupted. We are unable to find satisfaction and fulfilment in work. We are unable to handle our responsibility for others and for the environment. All this results from the broken relationship between humanity and the God who made us, knows us and loves us.

The Bible could have ended in Genesis 4. (Being a lot shorter, everyone would know it much better!) In pronouncing the curse on Cain, God would be seen to have acted justly and there would be no grounds for complaint. The biblical record would be desperately sad, but, as a statement of why things are the way they are, it would be painfully accurate.

episode 3: God intervenes

The God of the Bible is not just a God of justice, but a God of amazing love. The Bible tells us that the God of the universe set his heart on rescuing humanity. He did not treat us as we deserve. Instead, he embarked upon the most audacious rescue mission ever conceived. 'God so loved the world that he gave his one and only Son, that whoever believes in him shall not perish but have eternal life' (John 3:16). God himself came and did what we could not do. Jesus Christ is God himself come to earth, God with us and God for us. His premature death on the cross was not a tragedy, but the triumphant fulfilment of God's rescue plan. The last words spoken on the cross were 'It is finished' – three words in English, but one in Greek. *Tetelestai* was the word used in legal documents of the day, signifying 'Paid in full'. The blood of Christ, shed for the sin of the world covers our sin. In Christ we can once more experience the life for which we were originally made. In Christ we can once more be God's friend. In Christ we can begin to learn to relate to each other in an easy and natural way. In Christ we can find new purpose – not only looking after the land, but building his kingdom across the whole earth, on into eternity. And in Christ we are given new responsibilities and a fresh mandate.

It is not just that Christ died to make these things possible; he lives to make them real. He prays for us now at the Father's right hand. He has sent his Holy Spirit to empower and enable us to live as God intended. 'He who began a good work in you will carry it on to completion until the day of Christ Jesus' (Philippians 1:6). God is committed to that process of change and growth in us. He is more committed than we can ever be. 'This is how God showed his love among us: He sent his one and only Son into the world that we might live through him. This is love: not that we loved God, but that he loved us and sent his Son as an atoning sacrifice for our sins' (1 John 4:9–10).

episode 4: the King returns

Jesus is going to return to judge the living and the dead, and to create a new heaven and earth where God will make his home with humankind. Jesus died not to make a way back to Eden, but to open up the way onwards to glory. What is in place at the end is more than was in place at the beginning. There is progress all the way through the Bible. Its story starts in a garden and ends in a heavenly city. It starts with a couple and ends with a community. It starts with people created to know God and ends with people redeemed to be like God. The future is more glorious than the past. When God created humankind in his image, he knew that we would rebel and turn away from him. He foresaw the cost of that rebellion in the death of his own Son on the cross. But he judged that the risk was worth taking, and the cost worth paying, to create a people who would be his people for all eternity.

I remember clearly the day I realized something of the enormity of what Jesus had done for me. His death on the cross had profound implications for my world, my life and my relationships. Love so amazing, so divine, demanded my soul, my life, my all. (Mike, 23)

God did not make a mistake. The gospel is not a contingency plan whereby God frantically tries to make the best of a bad job out of our stupidity and error. God made people with free will, and he knew what humankind would do with it. Faced with the appalling prospect of humanity's rebellion, and all the implications that it would have for the whole of creation, for us and for his Son, God was willing to go down that road.

This tells us a great deal about the nature of God. Religion seeks to define God's nature in terms of what we want him to be. But he is more than our perception of him or even the sum of all perceptions of him. God *is* – and we must discover who he really is and learn to relate to him on that basis. God is who he reveals himself to be throughout the Bible; from creation to incarnation. Throughout the Bible, God's amazing plan unfolds. Hopeless people are offered hope, dying people are given eternal life, people on the road to destruction are shown a glorious destiny.

We need to understand all four acts of the drama as a whole if we are to grasp what kind of people God intends us to be and what our destiny is. If we consider only the couple in the garden made to be one flesh, we cannot see (for instance) why Jesus did not get married, or why Paul says, 'It is good ... to stay unmarried' (1 Corinthians 7:8). It is only through taking account of all the markers that we are able to navigate the wasteland. We learn about life from creation and the fall and Jesus and the hope of glory.

This hope of glory is something that the early believers clearly looked forward to. They used to greet each other with the word Maranatha, 'the Lord is coming soon'. Sometimes we accuse people of being so heavenly minded that they are of no earthly use, but often the reverse of this is true; they are so earthly minded that they are of no heavenly use.

The most important questions in life are not to do with getting married, having sex, or producing children, but concern ultimate meaning and eternal significance. Where have you come from? Where are you going? What gives you value? What is really important? These questions can be answered only by God and with God, in the context of his new community.

It is true that the relationship between husband and wife – the relationship established at creation – is a vivid picture of the relationship God has with his people. The commitment, intimacy and unity that a couple can experience model the quality of relationship which God desires of us, not just as individuals, but together as his people. But this picture is not the final goal. The finished article is much better. The Bible starts with a couple and ends with a wedding – the wedding of Christ and the church. It is a feast to which all are invited, and in which all Christians will participate.

This has to affect the way we think about relationships. Marriage is not what we were created for; it simply anticipates the perfected relationship between God and his people in glory. This foretaste of glory is experienced not only in marriage but in friendship, fellowship, church and family. It is to our detriment that we regard exclusive couples as more attractive than inclusive community.

There is a place for you in this new community. This is where you can discover what it is to love and to be loved, to share your most precious self, to encourage, and to be encouraged to develop significant relationships. For many this will involve marriage; for others it will not. What is certain is that it's possible to miss out on the fullness of what God wants to give us whether we are married or not.

The challenge that faces the church is to be the community that God has called us to be. Hypocrisy and selfishness too readily characterize our life together and our relationships. Too many churches seem to value families over single people, children over the elderly, people who fit in and are easy to get along with over the lonely, the marginalized and the distressed. The subtle tones and harmonies that make up the music of God's community are muted by every act of thoughtlessness and selfishness. Too many people have come into our churches and have not been welcomed, included or valued. The key question that faces all of us in our church involvement and relationships is whether we are going to be part of the problem or part of the solution. It is far easier to point out what is wrong, and to complain from the sidelines, than to work for positive change wherever we have opportunity. The tragedy is not just that we fall short of God's standards, but that we accept and perpetuate this state of affairs so uncritically.

The Bible is quite explicit: there is truth which can be known. The truth is not a proposition but a person. Jesus Christ said: 'I am the way and the truth and the life' (John 14:6). This is a remarkable statement. Jesus did not claim to know the way but to *be* the way. He did not claim to understand the truth but to *be* the truth. He did not claim to have a few interesting insights on life but to *be* the life. These claims taken together are remarkable. They are claims to be God. They are exclusive, non-negotiable truth claims. Jesus himself is the way, the truth and the life.

If you are following some other way, you are going in the wrong direction. If you have accepted some idea, insight or opinion contrary to him, you are mistaken. If you proceed to live your life apart from him, you will not receive eternal life.

God wants to be the most important thing in our lives. He has come in to do what we were incapable of doing, and has thereby established a solid foundation for all our activities and relationships. Lasting significance and true worth are found in Christ alone. Perhaps your deepest need is not sexual, but spiritual. Do you need to get right with the one who made you and knows you and loves you? Without this true foundation, nothing of lasting value can ever be built.

checking the foundation

are you complete in Christ?

Are you a whole person because of your relationship with Jesus? Do you stand complete in him or are you waiting for a man or a woman to make you complete? Another person cannot deliver holiness, wholeness and integrity. God wants to be the rock on which our lives are built. There is a place in our lives for other people, but that place is not God's place. Do you spend more time thinking about what you do not have, than about all that you have been given in Christ?

are you secure in Christ?

What makes you feel safe and protected? If our security is in houses or people or savings, it is misplaced. Such things can make us feel safe, but only God can give us true security. The security that God brings can cope with every circumstance in life and death. 'The name of the LORD is a strong tower; the righteous run into it and are safe' (Proverbs 18:10).

are you content with Christ?

Are you in love with Jesus Christ? Are you pleased that he is with you in your circumstances? In my last year at university we had a fire in our flat. Most of our possessions were destroyed. At the time it seemed terrible. But, through those weeks, we realized that, although we had little, we still had Jesus; and that having Jesus meant that we had plenty. Contentment lies in appreciating who we are in Jesus and not comparing ourselves with other people.

are you excited by Christ?

When you meet a couple who have just got engaged, they talk non-stop about each other. They wave the ring repeatedly under your nose and describe every detail of it. It is exciting knowing someone as terrific as Jesus Christ. As a Christian you have an intimate relationship with a person of supreme authority, majesty, patience and love. He too is delighted to have this relationship with you.

What is the most important thing in your life right now?

What do you most look forward to in the future?

What is your relationship with God like?

What do you think the Bible has to say about sex, friendship and intimacy?

Jesus makes the critical difference.

6. understanding the truth

How many times have we been here
Down this never-ending road
Where I'm trying not to give in
And where I know I should not go?

You see, I'm committed to another lover
Like I've never seen before
He gives me everything I need
How can you give me more?

Can you give me what God gives me?
Can you make me feel secure?
Can you guarantee a life of love?
If you can I'll still need more.

We take us to the very edge
Where we can dream as lovers do?
I can't afford to give in now
And I can't keep hurting you.

Can you give me life eternal
Or make my heart miss a beat?
Can you take me up with the moon and stars
And dance upon the clouds?
Can you make my life complete?

Alison Holmes

This song expresses the conviction that God is far more important than any human relationship. If we make someone more important than God or put someone else in God's place, we are guilty of idolatry. Not only does this deprive God of his rightful place, but it puts our friend or lover in the wrong place. This is not a good situation for anybody. We may well accept the truth of this in theory, but still make the mistake when faced with a real person. Truth is not always something we find easy to accept.

why the truth is so difficult to understand

One of the problems with the English language is that the verb 'know' can mean either 'recognize' or 'understand'. We may say, 'I know that $E = mc^2$', or 'I know that John supports Manchester City', without really understanding these phenomena at all. Recognizing the truth is quite different from understanding it. A familiarity with the truth which has not developed into understanding creates an awareness which may affect behaviour, but does very little to shape character. People who are familiar with the truth may behave in a certain manner, but often their behaviour does not express their character. When asked to explain their actions, they have no response.

I talked to some girls from Northern Ireland who were very clear-cut about their standards of behaviour. 'We don't drink, we don't smoke and we don't have sex.'

When I asked them why not, they looked at me very strangely. 'We just don't. We are not those kind of girls.'

Jesus said that if you hold to his teaching as his real disciple, 'you will know the truth, and the truth will set you free' (John 8:31–32). The knowledge of truth that brings liberation is not familiarity, or superficial recognition, but understanding. 'Learning' the truth at this level is the key to life. At the heart of understanding the truth is a developing relationship of discipleship with the one who is the Truth. 'If the Son sets you free, you will be free indeed' (John 8:36).

An angry student came to me after an evangelistic lecture I had given. 'I object to you'; he said. 'I object to your brainwashing and to the absence of choice in what you say.' As he continued, it became clear that he was the one who was against the freedom to make an informed choice. My accuser wanted people to be able to choose, but only if they made the same choices that he himself had made.

I believe it is vital that people should have the opportunity to make informed decisions with regard to sexuality and relationships. I believe Christians should be the most enthusiastic people of all about ideas. If the truth is the truth, it will stand up to scrutiny. Truth is not true just because you would like it to be so, or because it reinforces your personal choices. Truth is true because it is *ultimately* true; there is nothing beyond truth against which its validity can be assessed. This is why Jesus' claim to be 'the truth', which we looked at in the previous chapter, is so important. It means that ultimate truth is found not in a set of propositions, but in a person. There is a standard against which all ideas and opinions can be evaluated and their truthfulness determined. Truth is not a question of sincerity; you can be sincerely wrong. Truth is not a matter of consensus; whole groups can be sincerely wrong! Truth is not a question of trusting someone's teaching; you can be mislead.

The opportunity to consider truth is bound to help promote informed decision-making. What the Bible says is either true or false, and this should be explored openly.

As part of my English literature course at university, we studied the Bible as literature. Each lecturer warned the class that some of us would find it very difficult to study the Bible objectively, because of our personal belief system. Those who were committed Christians would be unable to handle the content of the course, through narrow-mindedness and prejudice. Yet it was most striking how well the lecturers' comments applied to *them*, and to the other students on the course. Many of those with no Christian background or experience were extremely unwilling to look at what the Bible had to say. They had already made up and closed their minds.

More recently, a religious studies student told me that the other students on her course had all purchased copies of the Qur'an and the Baghavad Gita but had not bought a Bible. She could not explain their inconsistency. When people grow accustomed to the darkness, the light is bright in their eyes and their natural inclination is to shy away.

God has given us his Word, the Bible, as a lamp at our feet and a light for our path (Psalm 119:105). Both these functions are important. We need a light ahead to set our course by, but we also need illumination for our daily footsteps.

This became clear to me while staying at Rannoch School on the edge of a Scottish moor. Being far from any city, it gets very dark at night. I used to have to cross the playing fields to get back to the chaplain's house, where I was staying. The chaplain used to leave a light on outside his house, and also lent me a torch. If he remembered to leave the light on and I remembered to take the torch, getting back was easy. I could glance up to see where I was heading and look down to avoid the mud and thorns. If I had only the house light to guide me, I would get there, but would arrive rather dirty. If I had only the torch, I would avoid the hazards, but would frequently lose my sense of direction.

One night, I forgot the torch and was dismayed to discover that the chaplain had not left his light on. I started forlornly across the field, when to my great relief I saw a light in the distance. Thankful that the chaplain had remembered to switch the light on after all, I headed purposefully in that direction. The route seemed longer than usual. I struggled through a ditch and some bramble bushes, through dense undergrowth and muddy puddles. Eventually I arrived at the roadside beside the loch. Suddenly, I realized that the light I had been striding towards so purposefully was positioned on a fishing-boat in the middle of the water.

understanding the truth

In the absence of the true light we tend to follow whichever light is the brightest.

I meet many people who are doing their best to find their way in life, often following whatever light seems the brightest. Their greatest need is to recognize the true light. 'In him [Jesus] was life, and that life was the light of all men. The light shines in the darkness, but the darkness has not understood it' (John 1:4–5).

This relationship between truth and light gives us important insights into the character of Jesus Christ. He is the truth our hearts hunger for in a world of deception and lies. He is the light we desperately seek in a world of darkness and confusion. But the lies and the darkness are not just around us; they are within us. Afraid of exposure, we shy away from the one hope that can rescue us. We try to rationalize and justify our position, explain away our actions and avoid any challenge, and cling to our personal opinions.

One guy I met had never considered the person of Jesus before, and was intrigued to find out the truth for himself. He started to read John's gospel. While reading it, he found it difficult to believe in Jesus. After a while, he began to question why this was so. 'I believed in a lot of strange things,' he said. 'I believed in intelligent life on other planets. I believed in the Loch Ness monster. I believed in Partick Thistle Football Club – all of which are less substantial than Jesus. Eventually it came to me,' he continued, 'that the reason I was finding it hard to believe in Jesus was not that he did not exist. Instead, it was that I had encountered a real, living person who was making claims on my life. I was no longer struggling with the reality of Jesus, but with the cost of following Jesus.'

We can begin to understand the truth only within a relationship with the one who *is* Truth. Our natural inclination is to turn away from the truth and to want to do our own thing. It is this selfishness and self-determination that lie at the root of our misunderstanding of sexuality and relationships.

The challenge, then, is to work at developing a deeper understanding of the truth and to be willing to see that truth applied to every area of our lives. The truth of God is relevant to all people in all cultures at all times. It does not need to be customized or adapted, but accepted and put into practice.

The heart of the human problem is the problem of the human heart. Only God is able to fix our broken hearts and untangle our muddled minds. So what does God, who is truth, want to tell us about sex and relationships?

The Bible has a great deal to say on these issues.

a summary of the Bible on God, sex and relationships

During the Relationships Revolution tours around university campuses, it became clear that students were finding it difficult to hold together important biblical truths on sex and relationships in their thinking and activity. So we developed this summary of what the Bible has to say on the matter. It is not perfect, but it serves to make some useful points.

- God is good
- Sex is good
- God's blueprint for sex is right

God is good

Everything about God is good. Our very understanding of goodness comes from his character. He desires the benefit of his people. He rejoices with us in our joys and weeps with us in our sorrows. He is infinitely patient, kind, loving, generous and faithful. He does not treat us as we deserve. He is a God of grace and mercy and compassion. He is a father to the fatherless and a friend to the lonely. He is good in every way.

We live in a moral universe. There is right and wrong and there will be judgment. This morality is determined not on arbitrary grounds, but by reference to God's character. His nature determines what is right and wrong. In the Bible, the revelation of God's standards for us is inextricably linked to his character. The Old Testament law not only gives guidelines for human behaviour, but reveals God's holy character. It helps us to appreciate both the kind of lives that God wants us to enjoy, and more of his nature. The command, 'Do not commit adultery', for instance, is given not to deprive us of the fun of sex outside of marriage, but to enable us to enjoy the benefits of a secure relationship. It shows us that God places a high value on marriage and faithfulness because he himself is faithful and does not cheat on us.

sex is good

The statement that sex is good does not imply that everything associated with sex is good, but that our capacity for intimate relationship, and for its physical expression in the proper context, is God-made and God-given. He does not look at a married couple having sex and think, 'What on earth are they doing? Who showed them how to do that? That's disgusting!' He made us as sexual beings, and our sexuality is far more than our capacity for physical intimacy. Sexuality is not satisfied or expressed through genital activity alone. This capacity to know and to be known, to express ourselves through our bodies, and to communicate appropriately, is good. God looked at the naked sexual beings he had created and saw that they were very good (Genesis 1:27, 31).

God's blueprint for sex is right

God, who made our sexuality, has given instructions on how it is to be used and enjoyed. This blueprint is like an architect's drawing, showing how something is designed to be. Because it is God who has given these guidelines, we know that they are right, because he is good, he made us, and he understands us. He has made it clear that sexual intercourse is to be reserved for marriage. This means that premarital, extramarital and homosexual intercourse are all proscribed behaviour.

God is good ... sex is good ... God's blueprint for sex is right. Misunderstandings tend to arise when people fail to hold these three things in tension. Many try to customize the truth by accepting only two parts of the summary, in various combinations.

'I believe that God is good and sex is good; therefore the blueprint can't be right.'

Some people affirm that God is good, and know from their experience that sex is good, but want to dismiss or redefine the Bible's 'repressive' teaching on sexuality. Biblical morality is seen largely as a matter of historical, cultural norms, which are inapplicable in today's society. This is where groups such as the Gay Christian Movement are coming from. It is also the stance of many Christian young people in the churches today.

But the blueprint is not culture-bound. The emphasis on monogamy, on commitment in relationships, on security, on the use of freedom with inbuilt safeguards for partners, children, families and society, should not be lightly dismissed. God's intention for our sex lives is not just a question of proof-texts. Because commitment and faithfulness characterize God's dealings with his people, they should characterize our relationships too.

'I believe that sex is good, and I'm willing to accept that biblical morality is God's blueprint for sex, but in that case God cannot be good.'

Some people know that sex is good and are willing to accept the Bible's teaching about it at face value. This leads them to the conclusion or suspicion that God cannot be good, because he wants to deprive them of sexual rights and freedoms. When the media portray the devil as sexy, horny and fun, they reinforce this stereotype – that God is not good, because he is opposed to sex.

But the guidelines God has given us do not contradict his goodness, but express it.

'I believe that God is good and that God's blueprint for sex is right; therefore sex cannot be good.'

There have been people throughout the history of the church to the present day who have adopted this line. They reason that God in his goodness has put restrictions on the use and enjoyment of sexual behaviour, because sex is not good. Sometimes this notion has been accompanied by anti-women propaganda; sometimes it has been fos-

tered by a reaction to the excesses of a particularly sensual society.
Some major figures, such as St Augustine, have seen sex almost as a
necessary evil in the procreation of children. But celibacy should not
be a negative thing, denying the goodness of sex, but rather a creative
and positive way of redirecting our sexuality. Certainly, sex can be mis-
used and abused, but it remains something that God has ordained and
made. In the middle of the Old Testament is a remarkable book called
the Song of Songs. It is impossible to read this sensuous love poem and
to draw the conclusion that sex in the Bible is not good.

why did God give us the blueprint?

In trying to understand the truth, it is vital that these three elements
– a right view of the goodness of God, a positive view of sexuality,
and a commitment to God's blueprint as revealed in the Bible – are
held together. You may be willing to accept this threefold truth, but
do you understand it, and do you believe it? If God is good and sex
is good, why does his blueprint place restrictions on the use and
enjoyment of sex? Take a few minutes to jot down as many reasons
as you can think of.

Perhaps your answers include words like 'safety', 'security', 'health'
and 'well-being'. These words speak of God's *protection* for us. Perhaps
you also thought of words like 'opportunity', 'blessing', 'fulfilment' and
'enjoyment'. These ideas are part of God's *provision* for us.

God's law functions like the lanes in an Olympic swimming final.
These lanes are there to keep the competitors on course and to
protect them from collisions, foul play or interference. The lanes
would get in the way only if someone tried to swim *across* the pool.
Similarly, God's law is there to keep us on course to win the prize,
and to protect us from harm.

God's provision and protection extends to all areas of our lives,
covering our physical, emotional and spiritual well-being. You might
like to think about some of the ways in which God's blueprint provides for us and protects us, as set out on pp. 64–65. There are many
good reasons why the plan God has given makes sense. What difference should this make to the way we live.

Physical	Emotional	Spiritual

HIV and Aids
unwanted pregnancy/abortion
56 known STDs
increased risk of cervical cancer
addiction to sex
loss of respect for the body
sin against your own body
(1 Cor. 6:18)
	feeling used
	disappointment
	losing part of yourself
	feeling just an 'object'
	insecurity
	loneliness
	mistrust
	fear of rejection
	guilt
	bad memories
	increased pain of break-up
	selfishness
	misunderstanding
	sex-dominated relationship
	loss of self-esteem
	feeling cheated
	loss of dignity
	comparison with previous
	    partners
	emotional trap
	marrying the wrong person
	emotional instability
	low view of other people
	resentment and bitterness
	emotional manipulation
	boredom
		dishonesty with God
		guilt and shame
		dishonouring God
		1 Cor. 6:19–20)
		God's judgment (Heb. 13:4)
		unhelpful influence on others –
		    Christians and unbelievers
		loss of meaning of the sexual act
		a wrong relationship continuing
		    when it would otherwise end

Protection		

64

Provision		
healthy life for you healthy family in the future sex as it was meant to be – more fulfilling sex within marriage	healthy self-worth growth of a deep and healthy friendship building of trust between you respect for each other good communication growth of deeper, truer love opportunity truly to give to the other person selfless expression of love growth of emotional maturity time for mind and body to mature specialness of marriage guilt-free sex in marriage opportunity to plan a marriage and family	healthy relationship with God growing ability to trust God our worth in God's eyes easier to accept clear conscience ability to support and encourage each other ability to minister effectively to others developing fruit of the Spirit – patience, self-control, etc. greater reliance on Christ for our worth, security, etc., therefore ultimately a more fulfilled life

7. friendship

Friend – *Noun* 1. A person with whom one is on terms of
mutual affection, independently of sexual or family love.

Oxford Paperback Dictionary

a famine of friendship

We live in an age where very little value is placed on friendship. So
few appreciate it because so few really experience it. We have
acquaintances, colleagues and neighbours, yet many of these contacts fail to develop into meaningful friendships.

The triangle formed by the three main aspects of our lives –
home, work and leisure – has expanded. We cover more miles in
the course of our daily lives. At the same time, opportunities for regular contact with others have got smaller. We see one set of people
at work and another when we go shopping. We hardly ever meet
our neighbours, and tend to know little about those we do. The
church, which could be a focus of community life, often buys into the
commuter culture, with people travelling long distances to worship
with another distinct group of people.

Training and careers demand our time and may move us geographically every few years. The busyness of life can leave little time for investing in friendship. What little disposable time we have is often taken up pursuing romantic relationships, maintaining family contact and finding our own space.

Low self-esteem has become an epidemic. 'Why should anyone bother with me?' we think. This makes us reluctant to initiate friendships or scared of developing them. There is a fear of forming ties which may then be broken by circumstance or betrayal.

We find hypocrisy in ourselves and in others as we play the game of trying to be the kind of person we think they will like and do the things we believe they will approve of. This is a game we cannot win.

Many go through life with a sense of being surrounded by hordes of other people, but connecting with precious few. Good role models and examples of friendship are lacking. Many of the relationships we see as being the most valuable are those that contain elements of sexual or family love. Sometimes we put so much time and energy into these relationships that we neglect friendship. David meets Julie and finds in her a kindred, caring spirit. This kind of intimacy and enjoyment of someone else is largely misinterpreted by our culture as sexual. The couple may be confused themselves, so they go out too soon and often go too far physically and emotionally. The relationship doesn't work, and is succeeded by another. These numerous and prematurely intense relationships which young people pursue are often unhelpful in developing an appreciation of friendship.

We tend to be suspicious of real friendship. A friendship between two people is suspect; exclusivity must mean secrecy of some sort, possibly sexual. Larger groups of friends are often seen as a clique or as a power base from which to challenge the leadership or the status quo.

The Bible has a very high view of friendship. God does not want us to experience a famine of friendship, but to enjoy a feast. In fact, those who have been forgiven he calls his friends (see Exodus 33:11; John 15:13–15; James 2:23). Throughout the Bible we see many

friendship

models of good friendships in action. Jesus had many friends during his life on earth, both men and women. Much of the New Testament is written by a group of friends. Several of Paul's letters are written with friends, to friends. The history of the church is characterized by friends working together for the gospel.

Perhaps one of the best biblical examples of friendship is that of David and Jonathan. We'll look at their story now.

a model of friendship

Jonathan became one in spirit with David, and he loved him as himself ... And Jonathan made a covenant with David because he loved him as himself. Jonathan took off the robe he was wearing and gave it to David, along with his tunic, and even his sword, his bow and his belt. (1 Samuel 18:1–4)

This friendship begins after David's defeat of Goliath, the gigantic Philistine. Something clicks between the young prince Jonathan and the young hero. Jonathan is no stranger to doing battle with the Philistines himself, having killed twenty people with the help of his armour-bearer, and having been involved in the victory at Beth Aven (1 Samuel 14). There is something in David that Jonathan finds attractive, and *vice versa*. There is a depth and a mutuality in their relationship. It is a friendship that is going to mean a great deal to David. When eventually Jonathan is killed in battle, David's lament over his body expresses the magnitude of his loss:

> I grieve for you, Jonathan my brother;
>   you were very dear to me.
> Your love for me was wonderful,
>   more wonderful than that of women.
>
> (2 Samuel 1:26)

From their relationship we can draw out seven marks of real friendship.

1. mutual commitment

David and Jonathan become 'one in spirit'. It is stated twice that David loved his friend as himself. This is the kind of love Jesus spoke of when he said that one of the two greatest commandments is 'Love your neighbour as yourself' (Mark 12:28–31). This is not an exhortation to love yourself more so that you can love others more. The commandment encourages us to look after others as carefully and thoughtfully as we look after ourselves. We pay a great deal of attention to our food, to working out what is the best course of action for ourselves, and to spending our time and money for our own benefit.

The unity of spirit and depth of love between these two people of the same sex is very striking. It demonstrates that a high degree of friendship is possible in such relationships. Some have interpreted David and Jonathan's friendship as a sexual relationship. There is no hint of this in the Bible. The key to their friendship is not the unity of bodies but the unity of spirit.

2. sacrificial love

Jonathan gives David the best he has. His gifts are not spares or leftovers. The sword and the robe are symbols of his status and role. Jonathan is humbling himself and honouring David. In giving him his weapon, he is making himself vulnerable to his friend. David, in accepting the gift, is humbling himself and honouring Jonathan; David does not need a sword, for he has just won Goliath's. We see here a striking example of mutual humility, vulnerability and trust.

This kind of giving is a mark of true friendship. Jonathan could have felt threatened by David's achievement on the field of battle. He could have exerted his princely authority. But instead he chose to show honour and respect to his friend. Jonathan takes an initiative which is positive and deliberate – to build a friendship with David. Sacrificial love like this is going to characterize Jonathan's whole friendship with David.

Later, he helps David escape from the fury of Saul (Jonathan's own father!), and almost certainly saves David's life. In so doing, he assists in the process that leads to David becoming king, and so loses his own title to the throne. Sacrifice that promotes the good of the other is the cost of true friendship. Immediately before his flight, David 'bowed down before Jonathan three times, with his face to the ground. Then they kissed each other and wept together – but David wept the most. Jonathan said to David, "Go in peace for we have sworn friendship with each other in the name of the LORD, saying 'The LORD is witness between you and me, and between your descendants and my descendants for ever.'" Then David left, and Jonathan went back to the town' (1 Samuel 20:41–42).

3. openness and honesty

The course of David and Jonathan's relationship is not going to run smoothly. Saul feels his positioned threatened by David's success in battle, and tries to kill him. Jonathan and David are able to speak honestly and openly about this (1 Samuel 19:1–7). Honesty is a hallmark of real friendship. Friends do not pretend about themselves or others and do not desire or need to cover up their struggles or failings. The openness and honesty extend to Jonathan's dealings with his father; he is willing to mediate between him and David. A willingness to work for conciliation, to put your own reputation on the line on behalf of someone else, is another mark of true friendship. Friendship does not mean the avoidance of conflict; it proves itself in the resolution of conflict. The fact that people may never have had a row or a disagreement is not necessarily a testimony to the quality of their relationship.

4. service

When problems again develop between David and Saul, Jonathan can scarcely believe it; but he is willing to place himself at David's disposal. 'Whatever you want me to do, I'll do it for you,' he says (1 Samuel 20:4). This echoes the words spoken by Jonathan's own armour bearer: 'Go ahead; I am with you heart and soul' (1 Samuel 14:7). It underlines how good experiences of friendship can feed into other relationships down the line. Jonathan's willingness to do whatever David needs him to do is a mark of true friendship. He does not qualify his willingness to help; he does not lay down conditions; he simply offers to do whatever his friend requires of him. This willingness to take risks, to trust someone with our life, to be willing to do whatever he or she needs, is a mark of true friendship.

5. God-centredness

The storyteller keeps repeating that the relationship David and Jonathan enjoy is centred on God. Several times he mentions that they have sworn friendship together before the LORD (1 Samuel 18:3; 20:17, 42). They are willing for God to judge between them if they do not keep their word. They are conscious that God plays a role in their friendship, and each is concerned to see God's plans furthered in the life of the other. Sometimes we imagine that we need a partner of the opposite sex in order to become more godly. If we focus on this, we can neglect the possibilities and opportunities that our friendships can present here and now. This principle applies to all our friendships, whether we share the same Christian faith or not.

6. interdependence

David and Jonathan work out a plan whereby David can flee if necessary (1 Samuel 20:18–23). Its success depends on their both keeping their word and being in the right place at the right time. Friendship is not about making people dependent upon us, or about us becoming dependent on other people. Dependency is not a good thing. Interdependency, however, is. When we work together and trust each other, and help and rely on each other, true friendship can develop and grow.

7. willing to let go

Having sworn friendship, David and Jonathan part and go in different directions to follow the call of God (1 Samuel 20:42). They are willing to count the cost. Their friendship, although extremely important, is not the most important thing in their lives. Even their friend-ship is at God's disposal.

There are many great examples of friendship in the Bible – men and women who followed God's agenda in their relationships and had a significant impact in their culture.

When faced with the famine of friendship, the key question is whether we are going to be part of the problem or part of the solution. Are you ready to pay the price of being a good friend?

frie friendship

8. building friendship

One day a man was walking home when he heard a voice. 'Hello!' the voice said.

He looked round, but could not see anybody.

'Hello!' the voice said again. 'Down here!'

He looked down, and there, on a rock by the side of the road, sat a frog. 'Hello!' the man replied, somewhat surprised.

'I am a beautiful princess who has been put under a wicked spell,' explained the frog. 'But if you kiss me, the spell will be broken and I will be a princess again.'

The man looked unconvinced.

'Go on,' the frog urged. 'If you do, I will love you and stay with you for ever.'

'Have you got a picture of yourself before you were turned into a frog?' the man asked.

Being a well organized frog, she did. She took it out of her pocket and gave it to the man. Sure enough, it was a photo of a drop-dead gorgeous woman. So the man bent down, picked her up and put her in his pocket.

Hearing muffled complaints he took her out again. 'What do you think you're doing?' the frog asked. 'I thought you were going to kiss me.'

'Look,' he replied. 'I'm a busy man. I don't have time for a girlfriend. But a talking frog is pretty cool.'

And he put her back in his pocket and walked off down the road.

Many people, when presented with the risk and challenge of a relationship, actually do something similar. We choose to settle for the kind of relationship in which we are comfortable and in control. We think it is pretty cool, and often don't begin to appreciate how much more is on offer.

Real friendship requires work. The potential rewards are immense, but the investment is costly and there is an element of risk. How can we cultivate and encourage positive friendships?

be genuine

There is no need to change gear or pretend to be someone else when you meet and talk to people. Be sincere, tell the truth about yourself and don't pretend to be perfect or coping with life all the time. If you spend all your time pretending to be somebody else, who's going to spend all their time being you? You are a unique and special person; you do not need to package yourself to make yourself presentable. Be genuine and allow people to get to know the real you.

Having grown up in an area where there were more boys my age than girls and, being a bit of a tomboy, I've always found it a lot easier to get on with blokes than with members of my own sex. Although I did have some fairly close female friends as a teenager, it wasn't really until university that I established any really good same-sex friendships.

One friend in particular really helped me to see what a good friendship between girls can be like. Katy and I got to know each other towards the end of my first year. We had been members of the same drama group for most of that year, but she had been in a relationship with another member of the group and so I had only really known her as one half of a couple. When the relationship ended, however, I discovered that she was a person in her own right and someone I could get to know well. Our friendship grew out of our shared interests, faith and love of chocolate, and also from the fact that we were the same age, had a very similar sense of humour and were involved in the same activities at uni, though we were on different courses.

The friendship deepened further when I developed an interest in her ex-boyfriend and needed someone to talk to about any potential relationship. I also needed to gauge what her reaction might be. Though things didn't develop between me and the bloke in question, my friendship with Katy was firmly cemented.

One thing I learnt about friendship which was actually quite difficult for me was the need to be open and honest, to allow my friend to see the real me and to allow myself to become involved with her life. This means sharing the bad stuff as well as the good. I also learnt that friendship isn't something you can force. There were times when our workload or other friendships meant that we didn't see each other often. I had to learn that this didn't mean that our friendship wasn't important, but that it had to be flexible. (Siobhan, 23)

I have two good male friends I meet up with on a regular basis purposefully to share where we are at in different spheres of our lives – spiritual, emotional, relational, with families, with girlfriends and at work. We became close through telling each other about personal matters at different moments, and being vulnerable. We each separately yearned for good, open friendships where we were real and honest and telling it like it is with our friends. We shared our struggles sexually – masturbation, lust, struggles with sexual orientation, and so on. This was in the context of an increasingly closer friendship anyway – laughing together, talking about doctrine, taking the mick out of each other, being on the CU committee together, praying together (Owen, 24)

be curious

Be interested in other people. They are not there just to fill in the gaps in your life. They matter. Try to find out about what makes them tick. Ask gently probing questions, and listen to the replies; do not just think about what to say next. Try to ask open questions that will help people to talk, rather than questions requiring the answer 'Yes' or 'No'. Friendship involves not just discovering the facts about people, but also their attitudes and feelings. How have they changed? How are they changing? What do they most enjoy doing? What do they think about what is going on? How are they feeling?

This curiosity should also extend to spiritual areas of life. Are they Christians? What is stopping them becoming Christians? Or how did they become Christians? What are they reading and learning at the moment? How do they relate their studies to their faith and work? What do their friends and family think about their faith?

It may feel threatening to put some of these items on the agenda. Remember, whatever you ask about, you must be willing to talk about yourself.

be available

Make time for people. Many of us are so busy that we leave little time for others. But it is not a question of whether we *have* the time, but whether we are willing to *make* the time. Look for ways of involving other people in whatever you are doing. Mealtimes, travelling, shopping, walking, playing squash together – all these can communicate that you are available and willing for a friendship to develop.

be loyal

Are you trustworthy? Can you be trusted with secrets and personal confidences? Can you be relied upon to be there, especially when the going is tough?

The question of secrecy must be handled with care. It may not always be appropriate to promise complete confidentiality. We may need the freedom to discuss an issue with someone else, perhaps with our friend's permission. If people feel unable to talk to us on that basis, then they need not do so. But we need to make every effort to be as loyal as possible to our friends.

For a long while I didn't appreciate the value of my friendship with Mike. The past twelve months have seen a huge increase in my awareness of how important my friendship with him in particular has been, and more generally how vital true, genuine and deep friendship is. This is especially clear in a culture where friendship, like everything else, seems to be disposable. (Andy, 23)

include others in existing friendships

An important way of involving new people in friendship is to ask them along to meals and outings and coffee invitations. If a group of you are going to the cinema, invite someone to join you. People who are lonely or marginalized often find it easier to join a group of friends than to be adopted as a project by someone who wants to look after them.

break down barriers

Friendships can easily become ghettos. Friends tend to be people of the same age, background and interests. It is worth trying to cultivate friendships with people who are different from you. Perhaps you could get to know people from different ethnic backgrounds or cultures; people from overseas who have come here to study or work; or people of different ages in your church or workplace. What are the issues that affect a man about to retire, or a young working mother? You may be surprised by how much you can learn and receive from a wide variety of people. Sadly, we can be very short-sighted when we look around for potential friendships.

pray

The apostle John made three prayer requests for his 'dear friend' Gaius: for his health, for his everyday life to prosper, and for his walk with God to progress (3 John 2). What do you pray for your friends? It is good to pray for their ups and downs, and for their granny's operation, but do you also pray that they will grow and mature in Christ?

My strongest friendships are the ones where we talk about God, where we can pray together naturally when things come up. Accountability in our relationships with God brings us closer together. Phoning, talking or writing to each other even briefly takes time and effort, but it is vital. Knowing we are open to talk to each other about deep questions spurs us on. I have had to work at my friendships, making sure I spend a lot of time with a few rather than little time with lots of people. (Sheila, 23)

be brave

Friendship of this quality does not come easily or cheaply. We shall make mistakes, we shall be hurt, and we shall hurt others; but if we are going to achieve the heights that friendship offers, we must be willing to take risks. Like us, other people are not perfect, and make mistakes. That is why repentance and forgiveness must be the normal pattern in all healthy relationships.

Coming to uni meant leaving behind all previous supports. I was quick to get involved in the small CU and to get to know another guy there whom I'd met briefly once before, as we were from the same city. We discovered we had similar beliefs and church backgrounds, and shared a sense of humour. We found ourselves in many of the same classes too. Feeling keenly the need for care and support, we decided to meet and chat and pray together. We quickly became committed to weekly prayer and Bible study, especially praying for friends of ours who weren't yet Christians.

The friendship developed as we made conscious decisions to work at and bear with our friendship, seeing it as a key point in our shared growth in the faith while at uni. In practice, this meant adopting an open and vulnerable attitude as we talked through emotions, interpersonal problems and stresses together, and didn't shrink from confronting our frictions with each other. Having grown together and become alike, frictions and tensions were common, but they were never serious. They were easily confronted because we knew we could talk about them openly and at ease. (Jason, 24)

be a good friend

When I was fourteen, our family moved to a new area, and that meant a change of school and friends. At my new school, people had known each other for a while and had formed their own friendship groups. They welcomed me, but I still felt insecure and lonely. I felt no-one understood where I was coming from, and I lacked confidence to be myself. I always knew a lot about other people, but they never knew much about what was going inside me.

When I went to university I really appreciated the fact that everyone was starting at the same time. No-one knew each other, and I had the chance that I hadn't had in school to make new friends at the same time as everyone else.

It was at university that I met Victoria and Rachel. Victoria was in the same hall as me and we were excited to discover we were both Christians. What struck me about her was her openness. She was very 'giving' in her friendship with me, and I felt she accepted me for who I was. She encouraged me to come out of my shell. Rachel too proved to be someone I can trust. I know I can tell her anything and she won't reject me. She has stood by me and cared in some hard times. She's tough on me when I need it, and gives me sound advice.

I have laughed and cried with these people. They have shown me acceptance and love. We've grown together as we've helped each other. They were my first two friends and I hope they always will be my friends.

I know, though, that it is not just their friendship that has helped me and changed me. It's God. As I grew as a Christian at university, I started to see that my security and self-worth as a person should come from him, because of what he has done for me and because of who I am in him. Seeing myself from God's perspective has given me confidence and security. ❯ (Kirsty, 22)

be accountable

In a relationship of accountability, we give each other explicit permission to ask questions about our lives. This is not compulsory in Scripture, but it can be a useful way of putting some scriptural principles into practice.

Here are some ways you can help each other grow.

confess your sins to each other

We must confess our sins to God and ask for his forgiveness, but it can be helpful to confess our sins to each other too, perhaps before or during prayer. This often results in a stronger assurance of forgiveness.

teach and challenge each other

'If your brother sins,' said Jesus, 'rebuke him, and if he repents, forgive him.' We are to rebuke each other, not to break each other down, but to help each other become more like Christ and to build each other up. We are to rebuke, not attack each other. We are to do it out of love, not out of malice or envy. Our sincere desire should be that our friend will repent and be restored and forgiven.

It is worth examining our own heart first. Are our motives the right ones? Are we living a holy life, as we will be urging our friend to do?

We need to affirm our commitment to the person before we issue the rebuke, and to approach the matter gently and sensitively inviting dialogue. We should raise the subject in private initially, and draw in others only if the rebuke is not heeded.

We benefit a great deal when people are willing to say hard things

building friendship

to us. As we give and receive teaching and challenge, we mature and grow.

ask each other questions

A friend of mine uses the following checklist in an accountable relationship. The deal is that on Monday mornings his friend asks him these questions:

— How has your Bible study and prayer been going, and how do you feel about that?
— What encouraged you most last week?
— What did you watch and read last week? When were you conscious of thinking unhelpful thoughts?
— Who and what have you been thinking, dreaming or fantasizing about?
— How have your relationships with people been going at work, home and church?
— How is your relationship with Rachel [his wife] going? What is concerning and encouraging you spiritually, emotionally and sexually?
— What mistakes have you made and how have you handled this?
— What did you spend money on last week? Is there any expenditure you regret?
— What opportunities have you had to share your faith, and how did you use them?
— How can I be praying for you this week?

'I find it very helpful to submit myself voluntarily to this accountable relationship,' says my friend. 'I find it keeps me on my toes. It helps me to intercept sin and disorder at an early stage, and to fulfil the calling I believe God has given me.'

The questions on his list relate to particular issues in his life. Each of us would write different questions. You might feel appalled at the thought of somebody else knowing about your 'private' actions and thoughts, especially if they are a bit dodgy. But what is wrong is not the fact that your friend knows about it, but that you are doing it. In our own private world, we easily fall into the trap of justifying and rationalizing our behaviour, but naming our sins and failures, and bringing them out into the open, helps us see them for what they really are. Being vulnerable can allow others to support us and enable us to see the necessity of change for ourselves. Other people can also help us to appreciate God's forgiveness by pointing us to relevant Bible passages and emphasizing God's promise to forgive.

A word of caution. We must beware of the dangers of becoming dependent on our friend and of encouraging dependency; of manipulating our friend; and of friendships where sharing problems becomes a substitute for commitment to growth.

Do you know somebody with whom you could establish an accountability relationship? If not, is there somebody you could get to know better by forming a prayer partnership, with the hope that this might develop into an accountability relationship later?

These relationships do not have to last for ever. We may choose to make ourselves accountable to a particular person on a specific issue for an agreed period of time. This kind of accountability is often a good place to start. Many have found that accountability has been the key factor helping them to move forward in the whole area of sexuality.

beware of pitfalls

Friendship can be fragile. Even good friendships can experience difficulties from time to time. Here are three particular pitfalls to beware of.

1. *Unrealistic expectations*. People sometimes expect friendship to be exclusive. They expect to spend all their time with their friend. This can give rise to frustration and jealousy. Friends are not there just to fulfil our needs, but have a life of their own. If we care about them, we will not resent this, but will rather be genuinely interested in their other activities, colleagues and friends.

2. *Unresolved conflict*. Where a problem does develop, it is tempting to ignore it in the hope that it will go away. As we noticed when

we looked at the friendship of David and Jonathan, quality friendship is not determined by the absence of conflict, but by how it is resolved. Talk through the issue and take time to listen. The quirks and failings that frustrate us about our friends often frustrate them too. It is easy to imagine that our friends are oblivious to their faults, when actually they are all too aware of them.

Sometimes conflict is based on misunderstanding. We can interpret facts as we understand them and come to wrong conclusions. As we listen, we must be willing to change our perceptions where we have been wrong.

Sometimes we might need to ask someone else to help us resolve the situation. This is not a sign of weakness, but a mark of maturity. If you care about your friendship, it is worth taking the risk of trying to sort things out as best you can. When conflict is resolved, the previous level of intimacy may well be restored or deepened, but sometimes it may become apparent that the friendship cannot continue on the former basis. Even though you cannot determine what the outcome will be, you must be committed to resolving conflict early.

Tim and I are very different. He is an extrovert and I am an introvert. He is a very straight talker, with no holds barred; but I wanted him to be 'nice' to people and not so threatening and outrageously upsetting. I often felt I had to pick up the pieces after he had said some damaging things. I was basically trying to make him more like me! He wanted me to be more like a previous friend, solely committed to the friendship with him. These two tensions (he trying to make me more like his other friend, and I trying to make him more like me) started to affect our friendship. It seemed to be falling apart. We would often snap at each other or make hurtful or back-handed remarks in passing.

We both became increasingly aware of this. He decided to sort it out. He asked an older acquaintance, whom we both knew, if she would help us to talk things through. She acted as negotiator, and it really helped. All these underlying tensions were brought to the surface. We both saw what pressure we were placing on each other. We got a lot of hurt out into the open, and realized how the relationship had got to where it was. We determined to accept each other more, recognizing the differences. We could even see them as an advantage as we each learned what the other was doing and how each of us was thinking and being. We also appreciated how much common ground we had in Jesus, and how foolish it was to let lesser matters get in the way of what was a beneficial and encouraging relationship in God. (Nigel, 24)

3. *Unfulfilled potential*. Instead of encouraging our growth to maturity, our friendships can develop in such a way as to stunt it. Without intending it, we develop patterns of talking and relating in which some subjects are acceptable and others are neglected. Even between friends who have enjoyed a deep level of sharing in the past, it can become increasingly difficult to talk about things that matter. Friendships that are increasingly characterized by selfishness, self-interest or superficiality can quickly become a hindrance rather than a help. It is worth taking stock of our friendships periodically, evaluating together where they are going.

be supportive

Someone once said, 'A friend in need is a liability.' We get used to meeting our friends to relax, have fun, and enjoy each other. When somebody in the group begins to struggle, it can be difficult to cope. But we all need extra support at times. A friend may go through illness, stress, bereavement, unemployment or spiritual dryness, or be dealing with particular issues. The way we approach these times will prove the true depth and value of our friendship. If we stand with others in their times of trouble, we may well discover that, when trouble comes our way, we are not alone. It is particularly important to try to provide and receive support in the context of a *group* of friends. This spreads the burden, helps avoid dependency on one person, and strengthens the group.

building friendship

Perhaps the biggest lesson I learnt from my friendship with Jackie concerned the issue of balancing friendships with relationships. When she began going out with a mutual friend of ours, this meant an adjustment in our friendship. A year later, she got engaged to the guy, who was by this time one of my housemates. What impressed me was the way our friendship was maintained alongside this relationship. I was never made to feel a gooseberry when spending time with them. I also learned to give them space to develop the relationship without resenting being left out. Having previously viewed same-sex relationships as difficult and in some ways unnecessary, I came to see (through this and other friendships) that we need to develop and invest in friendships with members of the same sex as well as with those of the opposite sex. They can be so valuable. The encouragement, support and love I have received through these friendships has definitely helped me in my overall growth as an individual. (Paula, 22)

going out
out

out

9. going out

Maybe I am bitter. In fact I know I am. After a string of disastrous relationships which have left me an emotional wreck for weeks on end, I am always filled with astonishment at my ability to go back for more time and time again. Shouldn't I have learned by now?

Oxford University Newspaper, January 1997

The search for love is translated into a complex set of dating rituals which leave many people hurting and bruised. It's not going out that's wrong; it's the way that we in our society choose to go out that is profoundly unhelpful.

There are two key issues here: finding a partner, and the ever-widening time-gap between puberty and marriage.

finding a partner

The search is on for Mr or Miss Right, the person with whom you will settle down, buy a house, have children, and grow old. Finding this important person was once the preserve of the family, or a matchmaker. The decision was out of the individual's hands. Now, we are left to sort this out ourselves. We hold self-determination in such high regard that even asking for advice goes against the grain. We are encouraged not to ask questions, but blindly to follow our feelings. Our hormones become our guiding star, from our mid-teens until our dying day. In Britain, the legal age of consent for heterosexual intercourse is sixteen. This is an age at which you are still considered too young to be in sole control of a car, to buy alcohol, to have a credit card or to vote.

Even when we are older, there is little help on how to find a partner. We are left on our own to make decisions that potentially affect all our friendships, our future and our whole life. The episodic nature of these relationships can sometimes makes us cynical, or more prone to entering too lightly into the next liaison. Disappointment teaches us that we cannot really trust ourselves. Love is a lottery, and when our number comes up we might as well enjoy ourselves while we can.

earlier puberty, later marriage

We live at a time when puberty is happening earlier and marriage later. Nobody completely understands the biological reasons why puberty is getting earlier. The economic and social reasons for marriage getting later are more easily catalogued: we want to enjoy ourselves, experiment with relationships, establish ourselves in a career and build up some assets before taking on a spouse and family. The result is a bigger time-lag than ever before between sexual maturity and what is considered an appropriate stage in life to 'settle down'. This has the effect of making 'going out' a state in itself. What would historically have been part of courtship, a prelude to a long-term relationship, has become an end in itself. We go out looking for Mr Right, but are quite willing to settle for Mr Right Now. The question of a life partner is a different matter that seems a long way away. Even engagement can become an interim state. Sometimes I ask newly engaged couples when they are getting married. 'We don't know,' they say; or 'Perhaps in a few years.'

We have developed a pattern of relationships which are public knowledge, intimate and exclusive, but short-term. When two people get married, everyone knows about it and understands the nature of the commitment. The promises are public and there are witnesses present. These witnesses are a legal requirement, and it is in fact their presence which makes the commitment public. Marriage is a public commitment with public vows. Going out is a public commitment with private vows. When we go out with someone, everyone knows about it, but there is a great deal of ambiguity about the nature of the commitment. Going out can mean very different things to different people. Some consider themselves as good as married; others as 'engaged to be engaged'. We have been left on our own to work out for ourselves what the commitment means, and there are as many definitions as there are people.

what is 'going out'?

Why do we 'go out' with people? What are appropriate expectations and standards for people going out? These stories give glimpses of some of the issues involved.

At university I had many friends, both male and female. One of my closest friends was a guy called Stuart. My friendship with him developed during my second year. In my third year I shared a house with him and four others, so I now had more of a chance to spend time with him and get to know him better. It didn't help matters that rumours were flying about the extent of our friendship: were we going out? We didn't do too much to dispel the rumours, and in fact spent even more time together. Most of the time when we were in the house together was spent in each other's rooms. Alone together.

The friendship changed when he started being quite tactile and physical – not kissing or anything like that, but subtle stuff like holding my hand. I didn't complain, because it was quite nice and secretly I liked him a lot. This went on for a few weeks.

One day we went to a coffee shop in town and he sprang a question on me. Did I ever want there to be anything more to our friendship? Like a fool I told him the truth: 'Yes.' But, I said, I knew nothing would happen. He agreed with me, so that was that. Yet he was still tactile. This confused me, but I didn't question him.

Two weeks later I confronted him and asked him what he was thinking. He replied (get the sick-bucket), 'I think I'm falling for you.' We then discussed when would be the best time to start going out – now or final year. We decided to wait until after final year. OK, that was fine. I was on cloud nine. Somebody actually liked me; somebody found me attractive.

But then something went wrong. He came back from a long weekend at home and had turned into Mr Ice Man. Because of my shy nature I didn't push it in case he blew his top, but sort of accepted it.

Eventually it came out. He had changed his mind and would like to be just good friends. After that day our friendship went all pear-shaped. We didn't spend time together. We didn't talk, or if we did he was very flippant towards me, or else talked like a stranger. I think I cried myself to sleep for weeks after that. I had put so much of my trust in him. I had never felt so lonely in my life. It was never resolved. **)** (Pamela, 24)

(Tom was someone I met during a time when I was admittedly far from God. I'd stopped reading my Bible and praying, and had no desire for holiness whatsoever. He was a Christian, and lived with some of my friends. He'd recently started a new job. The moment I met him I fancied him. That sounds superficial, and I was! He was very good-looking with an Irish accent, and that was all it took.

A week later he came round to see me, and we ended up going out for a drink. We didn't really get on brilliantly, but it was quite clear that we fancied each other. We went to a club and ended up snogging. He walked me home and stayed the night at my house, in my bed. I had to get him up early, so that my Christian housemates didn't find out. I knew they would be shocked at the way I had behaved.

I was shocked at the way I had behaved. I had been out with several boys before, for several months each, and had never behaved like that before. Two of my ex-boyfriends had been Christians. I had never slept in their beds, and we had always set ourselves physical boundaries. I had never done anything more than kiss them. I had even been out with a non-Christian for a couple of months. I had stayed over in his bedroom, but our clothes had always stayed on, and all we really did was kiss. The guilt I felt about what had happened with Tom was great, but I also felt used, especially when his housemate told me that Tom didn't really like me or even fancy me much.

After a couple of weeks Tom phoned to apologize for the way he had behaved. I then saw him at a party, and we ended up kissing again. I stayed over at his house and we almost had sex together. This time I felt less guilty. The next time we went out he decided that he did like me. He stayed over and asked me if we could 'make love' – a phrase I found very out of place, seeing that love had nothing at all to do with it. By now Tom had decided that he did want to go out with me, but I couldn't do it. The guilt that I felt for the way I had behaved was so huge that it made me literally sick. I couldn't believe how close I had come to losing my virginity to a man who didn't even care about me, who definitely wasn't going to be my husband. I told him how I felt, and avoided him from then on. Staying away from him was the only way I could resist the temptation to be sexually involved with him.

Why did I behave this way? Why had the physical aspect in my relationships with my boyfriends not got out of hand in the way it had with Tom? The boys I had been out with previously I had cared about and respected. I had wanted to continue to respect them, and so had been careful not to lead them into sin. I had always been aware that, if I went too far with them physically at the beginning of a relationship, it would get difficult if we went out for a long period of time.

Tom and I didn't care about each other, or have any commitment to each other, therefore we didn't care if we treated each other badly. Also, I had met Tom at a time when I was lonely and had a low opinion of myself. I wanted someone who would fill a space in my life, make me feel wanted. But 'sex' could not fill the gap. In fact it reduced me to a mere object, making me feel used, and more unloved and unlovable than before. I now felt incapable of emotional intimacy, and suspected that many men would only ever think of me as a sex object. ❯ (Alison, 29)

❮ I came to my current relationship from a series of medium-term relationships – never single for more than a few weeks over the last five years. I was accustomed to sharing beds with my boyfriends. As a Christian, I didn't sleep with them, and attempted to persuade them that we shouldn't touch what we hadn't got, most of the time. As a result, I was looking forward to marriage as little more than a chance to let the man have what he wanted so he wouldn't hassle me so much.

After my first date with Sean, we went back to his house and talked and kissed till 5.30am. Then we decided it was time to sleep, so we got into his bed and turned off the lights. After a few minutes he said he wasn't happy with it, so I agreed to go home. We have now been going out for two years. We are in a relationship where to kiss and talk is to 'make love', and where we have never gone further than we agreed *together* (i.e. to stop whenever we felt lustful at all, and never touch what we hadn't got). I am so glad that we have never slept in the same bed, and now not even in the same house. I reckon if he hadn't been loving enough to ask me to go home, then this relationship would probably have gone the way of all the others. ❯
(Andrea, 25)

❮ I am in a good Christian relationship. We were first attracted to each other by our godliness. This surprised us both; we knew this is the way it should be, but hadn't imagined how it would work out in practice.

We talked a lot about what a Christian relationship would be – no snogging, as both of us had found this unhelpful in past relationships. We also agreed that we shouldn't go into it if we could see no possibility of marriage in the future. I would recommend talking about what a relationship is before much time has passed, so each can understand where the other is coming from and together apply biblical principles to it. We try to be wise with our use of time, learning from other couples that we should not forget our friends. We try to ensure we have a balance of group time and time alone together. We do not pray much together. I know people have different opinions on this, but we find it too intense, and the more spiritually linked we become, the faster the relationship moves on – physically it becomes more difficult.

The more time we spend alone together, the more difficult it becomes, too. I'm glad we have been ruthless about setting guidelines, otherwise we would be in all sorts of trouble now. Having God at the centre of our relationship means much more than praying or not praying. It's our whole attitude to the whole thing. It affects what we say and don't say, what we do and don't do, how we value each other, even how we value other people. If God wasn't in our relationship, we would probably still love each other, but it would be in a different way, probably a selfish way.
(Catherine, 24)

this could be the start ...

You meet a girl who you know could be *the* one. She makes your toes curl, your stomach knot, and your mouth go dry. You become even more of a gibbering idiot than you usually are. You are so incapacitated in her presence that you cannot ask her out. You decide that things will be better once you get to know her better, so you become friends. You become *best* friends – so good, in fact, that you can't bring yourself to ask her out. Yet there is this nagging voice in the back of your mind that says you could be more than friends. You swear that you will tell her how you feel. Then she tells you, 'I've met this really great guy ...'

principles in 'going out'

'Going out' is not easy. It is also a state that was not known in biblical times, when people were either unmarried, betrothed, or married. Yet the Bible has much to say about the way we are to relate to each other. 'Live as free men, but do not use your freedom as a cover-up for evil; live as servants of God. Show proper respect to everyone: Love the brotherhood of believers, fear God, honour the king' (1 Peter 2:16–17). 'Mostly what God does is love you – keep company with him and learn a life of love. Observe how Christ loved us. His love was not cautious, but extravagant. He did not love in order to get something from us, but to give everything of himself to us. Love like that. Don't allow love to turn into lust, setting off a downhill slide into sexual promiscuity, common filthy practices or bullying greed' (Ephesians 5:1–1, *The Message*).

'Going out' relationships should at the very least demonstrate the level of courtesy, consideration and sacrifice that God expects of all our relationships. To settle for a lesser standard and call it 'love' is fundamentally wrong. To pretend that in 'going out' relationships the normal rules do not apply is to sell yourself, your partner and the gospel for a little short-term self-satisfaction. The primary calling of a Christian is to live in a way that pleases God. If our 'going out' does not please God, then we would be better not doing it. The challenge, therefore, is to work out *how* we please Christ in our relationships, how we honour him as we 'go out', and how we love other people in practice. There is far too much casualness, self-indulgence, and unthinking selfishness masquerading as romantic love in relationships.

good reasons for 'going out'

1. 'Going out' is *a way of getting to know someone better*. It is not the only way, and it usually works more effectively when it grows out of friendship. When attraction is more than a passing phase, and there is mutual interest and the prospect of something longer-term developing, the way that you conceive of the relationship between yourselves can help trust to grow and love to develop. Knowing where you stand with somebody, and knowing that your partner is committed to you on the same basis, marks an important stage in the development of love. This special relationship, handled properly,

can be a tremendous source of joy, encouragement and learning. Even where it does not develop into marriage, we can take away precious memories and valuable experiences.

2. 'Going out' marks *an initial public commitment.* Learning to relate together . as a couple is not just about what the two of you do on your own. There is no such thing as a private relationship. Everything we do has implications for other friendships and for our families. The fact that other people know where you stand is a help as you test out this relationship. Again, much can be learned from being with other people when you are together. Shutting yourselves away as a couple will lay a poor foundation for any future life together. It deprives you of other people's involvement and robs them of your love. Too much of our 'going out' is done behind closed doors. This puts undue pressure on us and communicates to others that they have no part in this relationship.

When a third person is present with a couple, he or she may joke about playing the gooseberry: the person is getting in the way and should not be there. The origin of this phrase suggests something quite different. In Victorian England, courting couples would always be assigned a chaperone – someone who was there to look out for them and help the relationship develop. Sometimes a friendly chaperone would announce, 'I'm going to pick gooseberries.' Since this was frequently said where there were no gooseberries, or in the wrong season, to 'play the gooseberry' signalled a pretext for giving the couple a little time alone together. Today the pendulum has swung so far the other way that a moment when a 'gooseberry' is present seems to be a moment wasted.

This public aspect of 'going out' is important and should not be underestimated. Some people get so frustrated with the way the 'going out' culture operates that they attempt to bypass it completely. They move straight from friendship to engagement, or from friendship to elopement! This is not particularly healthy either. When possible commitment begins to be on your agenda and the nature of the relationship starts to change, 'going out' forms an important part of the testing and proving process by bringing it into the public domain.

bad reasons for 'going out'

1. Many people have a tremendous *fear of being 'left on the shelf'*. This can kick in at a remarkably early age. I have spoken with teenagers and young adults who have wrestled with this fear. During a talk at Oxford University, I once commented that it was quite possible that some of the students present would graduate without having met their life partner. Some were clearly horrified at this possibility. If they could not find someone during their student days, how would they ever?

I don't know where this shelf *is* exactly, but I do know that it is better to be on the shelf than to be locked in the wrong cupboard. At least on the shelf you can see life, and people can see you; you are available and can make a contribution. Fear is no basis for entering into a relationship. I know that it is difficult when you are desperate to be married, when every inch of your being screams out for companionship and when you feel like the last single person on the entire planet. Do not make the mistake, as many have, of clutching at straws. The fact that you do not have a partner does not mean that you are left on your own. Enjoy the friendships you have and work to develop them. If you cannot cope without a partner, you won't be able to cope with one.

2. *Peer pressure* can be very strong. A lot of teenage and young-adult culture revolves around being with a partner. When you don't have one, you feel left out. In later years, this feeling becomes most noticeable at weddings and work functions. Well-meaning friends sometimes try to pair you up with somebody 'suitable'. The pressure can be particularly acute when the circle that you move in is mostly paired up. But it is dangerous to let other people write the script for you. You only have one life to live. This is no dress rehearsal; this is the show. Don't let friends or family push you into a relationship that is not right for you. You are the one who would have to cope with the problems that would ensue.

3. The *lustful desire* to have somebody with whom we can express sexual feelings can be overpowering. If we are honest with ourselves, at that point we are not looking for *somebody*, we are looking for *anybody*. When the focus is on ourselves and our needs, desires and wants, our agenda becomes entirely selfish. This self-seeking, self-serving search is no basis for love or romance. Even meeting someone who is looking for the same outlet does not legitimize this misuse of our sexuality. Whenever we feel lust starting to take control, it is no time to initiate a relationship; it is time to head for the hills.

4. *Boredom* is no reason for 'going out'. If you are bored, you are probably boring. Get a life – *then* look for a partner!

5. Another faulty motive for going out is *to gain worth in the eyes of others*. We want to feel attractive and valued.

But you already have intrinsic worth and value as a person. You are not what you do, or what you have, or what others think you are. Your value does not come through associating with someone good-looking, funny and sexy. Your value as a person comes from God. You are made in the image of God, who has known you from your earliest days. He has demonstrated how much value he places on you by sending Jesus to die on the cross. You are worth a great deal.

Christians are people who have begun to appreciate the value that God places on them, who have become children of God, who have a living friendship with Jesus Christ, and who look forward to a glorious inheritance. A verse that helped me appreciate this is Zephaniah 3:17:

> The LORD your God is with you,
>   he is mighty to save.
> He will take great delight in you,
>   he will quiet you with his love,
>   he will rejoice over you with singing.

Many of our biggest struggles in life are actually theological. We need to see ourselves and others as God sees us. Sometimes we are tempted to put ourselves in the junk shop, slap a knock-down price on ourselves and be grateful when somebody buys. When we sell ourselves short like this, the buyer often has no sense of our true value and sticks us in a corner somewhere, or does not care for us as we deserve. There is a big difference between going out with somebody who appreciates our true value and getting into a relationship to seek value. The value we try to earn is always a lot less than the value we already have. The worth that God gives you is not theoretical; it is absolute and real.

10. getting relationships right

I wish I was me girlfriend,
Then I'd go out with me.
I'd like to be me girlfriend,
At least initially.

'Cos I would send me flowers,
And I would lend me books.
I'd even tape me records,
And comment on me looks.

I'd like to be me girlfriend,
Although I must confess,
As the relationship grew older,
I'd like it less and less.

I'd find it very puzzling,
I'd find myself confused,
When silent I'd stop speaking,
I'd wonder 'Was I used?'

When I'd finished watching me,
So wrapped up in myself,
I'd mourn me bad decision,
And climb back on the shelf.

Steve Ayers

take your time

There is no need to rush into a relationship or to develop commitment faster than is necessary. When you first become attracted to somebody, there can be an incredible sense of urgency to get things tied up and sorted out; but if the relationship is right for you, there is no rush. Your partner will still be the right one for you in a week's time or a month's time. You might be worried that he or she might meet somebody else in the meantime. If that happens and your partner decides to pursue that option, that just confirms that you might not be right for each other.

I do not believe that you have to marry the first person you go out with, but I do think that most people pass through too many relationships.

enjoy the other person

The person you are going out with is unique and special. There are all sorts of things about this person to know and understand. What are his interests? How does she see the future developing? Where do his gifts lie? How does she relate to her family, to other people, and to you in a group context? What is his relationship with God like? How strong is her commitment to serve? What motivates, excites and encourages him?

Going out with someone affords a unique opportunity to receive and give. Enjoy the experience and share yourself. The fact that you might get hurt in the future does not mean you should not take risks in the relationship you are in now. Even if you do wind up getting hurt, it does not mean it was wrong to take those risks. Commitment requires trust and necessitates risk. The privilege of

102

going out with someone also has responsibilities. Enjoy each other and build the right elements into each other's lives so that the future, whether it is together or apart, will not be spoilt by regret and bitterness.

relax about the future

The fact that you are going out with someone shows that you are serious about that person. The seriousness increases with age; it becomes ever more difficult to go for a coffee or take in a movie without appearing to present an offer of lifelong commitment. It is good to be serious about the future and not to enter into relationships lightly; but if you start asking serious questions about marriage and lifelong commitment early in the relationship, it can make you tense, distort your friendship and prevent it from developing naturally. Relax and enjoy the relationship for what it is. Going out is not the same as going out for a long time; going out for a long time is not the same as being engaged; being engaged is not the same as being married. Relax and appreciate each stage in the relationship.

keep it public

There is real value in spending as much time as possible together with other people. Many couples spend a lot of time behind closed doors. They develop a dual existence: when they are alone with each other they are passionate and frenzied, but in public they hardly speak to each other. Other couples take great delight in manifesting their oneness and exclusivity to the assembled company: eating Twiglets from opposite ends, holding hands continuously, wearing matching anoraks!

Work at having a relationship that is accessible to other people, that helps and benefits them, and that multiplies your effectiveness rather than detracts from it. Foundations are being laid here for whatever shape your relationship takes later. Learn to relate to each other's friends and families. See events like weddings and parties as opportunities to learn together. Take feedback from people. It takes work and effort to be able to relate naturally and well.

don't dump your friends

Friendship is not provisional. Friends are not people you hang around with until you find someone to go out with. People who thought they mattered to us sometimes are quickly marginalized or abandoned when we embark cn a new relationship. It is understandable to want to spend time with the person we are going out with, but it is foolish to abandon certainties in pursuit of possibilities. Friendships that have proved themselves over time should not be dismissed lightly or abused in this way.

It is also wrong, when you are going out with someone, to want to socialize just with other couples, so that when you are 'single' you do things with 'single friends' and when you are in a relationship you do things with other people in relationships. Our level of commitment to people does not depend on a relationship or lack of one.

Christian friendship, in particular, never takes the line of least resistance. It's OK to say that you are not able to go out with your partner because, for instance, you are seeing some friends. It is good for your partner to realize that he or she is not the centre of your life, that you had friends before this relationship, that other people matter to you, and that your partner is not the most important person in the world. God will always matter more than anyone, and your commitment to him entails priorities of sacrifice and service which you take very seriously. Other friendships are vital in maintaining our spiritual growth. Friends are people with whom we can pray, share, talk about spiritual things, and study the Bible. If these activities are concentrated in just one person, we make ourselves vulnerable. Stability and strength come from a network of meaningful relationships.

enjoy an appropriate level of intimacy

It is easy to become so dependent on someone that, if the relationship finishes, it leaves a disproportionately large hole.

Spiritual intimacy and sexual intimacy can get muddled up, to the point where the spiritual leads to the sexual. Spiritual intimacy can even appear to legitimize sexual intimacy. It is spiritually inappropriate to share everything in a 'going out' relationship. The fact that you pray together does not mean you should sleep together. Enjoy the attraction you feel towards one another, and acknowledge and appreciate your differences. Focus on creativity and intimacy, talking rather than kissing, serving more than touching.

The intensity of trying to fulfil all somebody's needs is not something that God asks of us even in marriage. Spiritual intimacy is great, but work at developing it in group contexts as much as possible. Go out as a group. Afterwards, discuss with friends what you have been thinking. Be at prayer meetings together; perhaps try to be in the same Bible study group or attend the same church where possible. Even in a long-distance relationship there needs to be a context for intimacy to develop. You cannot achieve it on your own.

Emotional intimacy is wonderful: being able to be open and share our deepest feelings, our past, the person we are, and our hopes for the future, without fear of being hurt or turned away. But beware of splurging everything too quickly. Time is the big test in any relationship. Commitment is demonstrated not through depth of feeling, but over the course of time, through ups and downs, changing seasons, mistakes, disappointments, joys and shared experiences. We learn to trust each other. We discover and grow together. Take is slowly. 'Guard your heart, for it is the wellspring of life' (Proverbs 4:23). That is not a call to be hard-hearted, but to be careful with our emotions. They are too precious to be exposed to all comers.

don't go too far

Setting appropriate boundaries is usually not a one-off decision, but a gradual process. The battleground is physical, but the level of emotional and spiritual intimacy too may be entirely inappropriate for the amount of commitment in the relationship. This testimony illustrates how we edge towards the danger zone by tiny steps:

I know I should have spoken sooner. Things are a real mess with my boyfriend. You might think that I couldn't help myself. It would be nice to pretend that I got carried away in the heat of the moment. But the truth is, I decided.

I decided to start imagining in my head what it would be like to be close to him.

I decided to invite him over when my flatmates were out.

I decided to sit on the bed together to watch a video.

I decided to let him sleep in the same room as me.

I decided that it saved any hassle.

I decided to get into bed beside him for a short while just to say goodnight.

I decided that I wanted to feel him close to me.

I decided that I wanted that intimacy.

I decided to let him undress me, touch my breasts.

I decided that it felt good that he liked my body, that he found me attractive.

I decided to allow him to guide my hand and show me what to do – what pleased him.

I decided in my head it was OK because the Bible didn't clearly say it was wrong.

I decided that as long as we didn't have penetrative sex it was OK.

I decided that my feelings of guilt were due to lack of experience and naïveté rather than conscience.

I decided to do it again another day.

I decided to undo his jeans to feel closer to him.

I decided it was OK to be naked together.

I decided to bring him to orgasm – to please him.

I decided that it wouldn't really matter as I thought I'd marry him.

I decided not to talk to anyone about it as I felt embarrassed and ashamed.

I decided that as long as he wanted me physically the relationship would last.

I decided to try to set some lines in the relationship.

I decided to give in because it was the easier option and it made me feel good.

I decided to stop repenting – it was only hypocritical.

I decided to go on holiday with him.

I decided to sleep in the same bed. I liked the security, the intimacy.

I decided to deceive my parents about our sleeping arrangements.

I decided that I didn't want to let go of what we had.

I decided not to talk to my friend when she asked about us.

I decided she wouldn't understand, and was scared of what she might think of me.

I decided the physical closeness was what I wanted most.

I decided not to go to church to give us more time together.

I decided it didn't matter if he didn't tell me he loved me; what he did to me was more important.

I decided it didn't matter if he hurt me, I would still love him and please him.

I decided it would be better to spend more time on our own together than with friends.

I decided to accept spending less time talking and more time arousing each other.

I know I should have spoken sooner. Things are in a real mess with my boyfriend. You might think that I couldn't help myself. It would be nice to pretend that I got carried away in the heat of the moment. But the truth is, I decided.

The decisions we make today affect the people we become tomorrow. The standards we adopt in the present lay the foundations for the decisions we will make in the future.

The best way to deal with sexual desire in a 'going out' relationship is not to focus on the problem, asking, 'How far can we go?' but to focus on contributing positively to each other's Christian life. What should we be getting on with that will build each other up, benefit other people and please God?

Try to think of as many elements as possible in your relationship to which you can give a *green* light. These are things you can really go for together.

- Christian service
- other friendships
- time together in groups

These are all positive things to be worked at and developed.

Many dangers come from spending too much time alone. This is all too easy as a couple. In addition to your own desires, other people may expect this of you.

Watch out for activities that need an *amber* light:

- spending less time talking and more time kissing
- spending too much time alone together
- praying together on your own
- planning and imagining situations in your head
- losing interest in other friends and relationships
- becoming less involved in Christian service
- needing ever more physical assurance
- becoming sexually aroused
- staying later and later in each other's accommodation
- choosing to wear provocative clothes

Red light activities should be stopped before you start:

- lying down together
- undressing each other
- staying over in each other's accommodation
- deliberately stimulating each other

Many Christian young people have a sex life. The issue is not just whether you are having penetrative sex, but whether you have a sex life or not. A sex life should be reserved for marriage. 'God intended sex to be a bonding experience as powerful as the bonding that takes place between a mother and a child at birth. If you constantly tear away at that bond, pretty soon you lose your ability to bond' (Julia Duin).

have a right view of sex and sin

Many 'going out' relationships adopt a relative approach to morality. People compare themselves to those around them rather than looking to God's standards. It is too easy to aim for mediocrity and to allow ourselves to sink to that level and become content with it. If we have wrong thoughts or behaviours, we must be willing to face up to them, and to make difficult choices.

talk things through with your partner

Discuss clearly what the relationship involves. 'I think I probably should tell you that I tend to be cautious about embarking on relationships and I need to take things quite slowly. It's important to me that we know where we stand and don't just slide into being unhelpful to each other.'

Talking is vital in keeping us on track. It is impossible to kiss and talk simultaneously. But in talking with a partner, don't fall into the trap of accommodating, over-explaining and being manipulated. Sometimes the thing to say is 'No'.

evaluate how things are going

Is knowing this person helpful for me (and *vice versa*)? Is this relationship helping me to grow, or leading me to compromise? Do we work well together? Are we growing in friendship? Am I deluding myself? Are we pleasing God in our relationship? Do we increasingly appreciate God's call on us, and is it taking us in the same direction? These are questions that we can properly answer only with the help of other people. We need to talk to each other, but not just on our own.

going out with someone who is not a Christian

All the above points assume that you are a Christian going out with someone who is a Christian too.

It was inconceivable to me that I would ever go out with someone who was not a Christian. Jesus was so important to me that being involved with someone who did not share in this friendship with him was impossible. My faith was not just a matter of preference or of interest; it was everything to me. I knew a number of women in our church whose husbands were not Christians, and I saw the conflict this caused in their use of home and money, and the way they brought up their children. I knew that light and darkness could not have fellowship together. I knew that I should not be unequally yoked with an unbeliever (2 Corinthians 6:14–15). All these things were clear to me, and I still agree with them all. Yet I find myself involved with a guy who is not a Christian. I never thought I would get into this position, and am not sure exactly how I did. (Sally, 20)

This testimony sets out the principle that Christians should only marry Christians. This is for the benefit of the couple, their families and the church community. (Separate instructions are given for the scenario where one partner comes to faith after marriage, but this is a different matter; I Corinthians 7:12–16.) Nevertheless people like Sally get into a position where an inappropriate relationship is leading to greater and greater commitment. The difficulty and compromise this brings are significant.

People who begin to go out with someone who is not a Christian usually justify their action by some or all of the following assertions.

'the person is really nice'

Of course the person will be nice if you are showing an interest! Some Christian young people grow up expecting not to be attracted to someone who is not a Christian. This is a fallacy. There are many nice, attractive non-Christians. The issue is not one of niceness, but of Christian commitment and spiritual status – whether or not the person has crossed over from death to life, from darkness to light. The distinction is as stark as that.

'the person might come to faith'

Everybody knows somebody who became a Christian in a 'going out' relationship. It is easy to believe that this might happen to you, your girlfriend or boyfriend too, particularly if she or he seems genuinely interested in coming to church and reading Christian books. But for every individual who comes to faith in this context, there are many more for whom the reverse happens. Instead of seeing the unbelieving partner come to faith, the believing partner compromises. If you are really concerned with somebody's welfare and eternal salvation, to get that concern muddled up with a romantic relationship is extreme folly. In many cases, the position is made worse in that the unbelieving partner only knows one Christian – you.

'the rules don't apply'

It is difficult to apply seemingly impersonal principles to a real personal relationship. Principles can seem unyielding and harsh. But God has given us guidelines for precisely those times of temptation when we are in real-life situations, faced with possibilities and opportunities that we find attractive and appealing. You may feel that you are an exception, that some reason makes your situation special or unique, and that it is OK for you because of the particularities of the individuals involved. But this desire for self-determination, this feeling that the rules were made for someone else, were at the heart of the first sin in the Garden of Eden. The serpent's opening move was to cast doubt on God's command ('Did God really say …?'), and his second was to assure Eve that she would be OK if she went ahead ('You shall not surely die') (Genesis 3:1–4).

'the rules don't matter'

'Does it matter that much if I am involved with someone who is not a Christian? We can work it out. My partner is very understanding, and supports me and respects my opinion.'

This sounds plausible, but it has the effect of putting someone else in God's place in your life. You cannot serve two masters. Once you start saying bits of God's Word do not matter, where do you draw the line? If you start listening selectively, how can you hear God speak?

'we're not getting married'

'There is still time for things to sort themselves out. I could not imagine marrying someone who is not a Christian, but we're not at that stage yet. What real harm is there in our present relationship?'

This is fair enough in some ways. We have already noted that the Bible does not address the issue of 'going out', because biblical cultures followed different patterns from ours. Nevertheless, in our culture, 'going out' does express commitment. Continuing to go out expresses a growing commitment, a deepening intimacy, an increasing dependence on each other. A desire to be together is rightly fostered and grows in such relationships. The possibility for self-delusion here is enormous. At what point in a relationship with a non-Christian is the level of commitment too great? How do you know when you are at that point? How do you know that you are not already beyond that point? How fair is it on your partner to enter into a relationship that you know has no future? How much guilt will you feel for having done what you knew was not right?

'my non-Christian partner treats me better than some of the Christians I have gone out with'

You may have had a bad experience with a Christian partner. You may have felt used and abused. Your family may like this person more than your Christian boyfriend or girlfriend. Your new partner may be more exciting, more interesting, more caring – or perhaps the only person on offer. But none of this is the point. Even when both partners are Christian, it is hard enough to live together and stay together, to be committed to each other, to seek God's help and provision together, to work together and share together, to bring up children and grow old together. All this presents significant challenges. How much more of a challenge will it be for partners whose lives are built on different foundations? Your opinion about this relationship has to take second place to what God desires for you.

Be rigorous with yourself. Have the guts to take a stand early on. If you have decided that you will only marry a Christian, it is better not to go out with a non-Christian. If you are not going to go out with a non-Christian it is better not to be interested in a non-Christian, or to flirt with a non-Christian, or to pursue a romantic friendship with a non-Christian. If you are in the middle of such a relationship now, it is not too late to make things right; but you will almost certainly need the help, counsel and support of those you can trust to stand with you.

splitting up

We tend to be better at starting relationships than at finishing them. Finishing relationships is often made harder by the fact that we have gone further than we should have done in them.

It is not appropriate to quit on a relationship just because things have become difficult. It is important to try to resolve difficulties, where possible, rather than just avoiding them. Working through difficulties can strengthen a friendship. We may need extra support to help us through this process.

Sometimes, however, it becomes apparent that the relationship has no future. The two of you are increasingly pulling in different directions. Rather than helping each other to grow, you are damaging each other. You are unable to keep your promises and commitments. Other people notice that you have become more selfish.

It is important to finish relationships well. In trying not to hurt each other, we may well fudge the issue and thus make a bigger mess. The situation is complicated if we have become attracted to someone else while in the midst of the existing relationship.

I believe it is particularly damaging to jump from one relationship straight into another. It does not give sufficient opportunity to sort through to the end of the previous relationship. It is hard on our former partner, and tends to make our relationships more self-centred: how *I* feel and what *I* want is the determining factor in how they develop and are resolved. It is much better to allow a few months after finishing a relationship before even thinking about starting another. That includes the preliminary stages, when you are still 'officially' friends but are moving towards going out.

One reason why we don't finish relationships cleanly is that we want to keep our partner hanging on as a back-up. We are not too happy about the way the relationship is going, but we don't want to risk being left with nobody. So we tell our partner: 'It's not you, it's me. I'm just not ready for commitment. Let's just stay friends and see what develops. I still really care about you. There's no-one else.' But the reality is: 'Listen, I'm quite immature. There is somebody else I'm interested in, but if that doesn't work out I might get back to you. Let's stay in touch.'

Being attracted to someone else may be a reason for finishing the relationship. In that case, it is wise to delay starting the new relationship for quite some time. Jumping from relationship to relationship is no foundation for a life of mature commitment. In time, you may be able to become friends with the person you used to go out with, but that will not be an instant or a seamless transition. Time is needed for wounds to heal and new relationships to develop. It is easy for motives to become confused, and for people to hold out hope that the relationship will resume when no such thing is intended.

finally ...

Going out can be great. We can have fun, grow and develop, mature in our attitudes and commitments, and experience the thrill of knowing and being known. A little bit of everyone we go out with stays with us for ever. But this privilege carries responsibilities. We cannot treat people as disposable toys, ours to play with as we chose. We must not pick people up, screw them up and throw them away. We must not enter into relationships lightly, or devalue or undermine the other person. Rather, we should try to develop good habits which will last a lifetime. Much of this will sometimes run contrary to what we want, to how we think and feel. But that is entirely the point. Our agenda for life and God's are not necessarily complementary. God's plan is not that his desires fit in more and more with ours, but that our desires fit in more and more with his. Relationships are a battleground, a testing-ground for faith. The need for radical discipleship here is as deep as in any other area of life.

We can be people who exemplify and model the highest standards in our relationships. We can live, not according to our own desires, but in line with the life that Jesus Christ died to give us. As we deny ourselves and take up our cross, we shall be saved from the banality, superficiality and indulgence that characterize many relationships. We desperately need this attitude if we are not to leave a trail of damaged people in our wake.

Be prepared to be different. Be prepared to take a stand. Tackle your relationships in a healthier way. 'Go out', but not according to the world's way. 'Do not conform any longer to the pattern of this world, but be transformed by the renewing of your mind' (Romans 12:2). The best relationships should help us glimpse that glorious renewal that awaits the whole of creation.

❝ What really helped us was deciding early on that, if we encountered any reason why we shouldn't get married, we shouldn't be going out. If I had made that decision in my previous relationships, we wouldn't have gone through the process of repeatedly breaking up and getting back together until we hated each other. We would never have been as cruel as we actually were. ❞ (Martha, 25)

I had been a Christian for a long time and was secure in my faith. But I wanted tangible security too; I wanted to feel attractive and accepted. I thought I would find this in a romantic relationship. I went out with a great Christian guy for eighteen months, but by the end of the relationship I felt less secure and accepted than before. I realized that no-one could give me absolute security, as they are needy people too. I also saw that what I'd been searching for had been available in Christ all along. Talking through issues of sex and relationships, thinking through the far-reaching effects of the cross and the reality of heaven, has given me real security, joy and freedom. I still experience moments of longing for acceptance in a human relationship, but now I feel equipped to give these feelings to God and to get on with living life to the full. (Judy, 26)

11. marriage and singleness

Men marry because they are tired: women because they are cautious. Both are disappointed.

Oscar Wilde

In Hollywood, all marriages are happy. It's trying to live together afterwards that causes all the problems.

Shelly Winters (attrib.)

Many quips about marriage contain a degree of cynicism. Marriage is not a word, but a sentence; it is an honourable institution, but who wants to live in an institution? Paradoxically, such definitions often surface in wedding speeches, hinting that the optimism and euphoria are tinged with wistfulness; the hope that the marriage will work out is tempered by the expectation that it won't. One UK marriage in three ends in divorce, but even those who are getting married for the second or third time cling to the hope that this time things will be different.

Our society portrays and perceives marriage as such a confusing mish-mash that it is difficult to work out what it is supposed to be about. In many respects marriage has got a bad name. It is worth considering some of the ideas about marriage which permeate our thinking.

marriage in our society
based on attraction

When we look for a partner we tend to survey the field on the lookout for the most attractive people, and follow our feelings. It is great to discover someone who is as attracted to us as we are to them.

The problem with marriage based on attraction, first, is that many of the features that attract us do not last. People's looks change over time, our personalities and characters develop, and we can discover that there is no longer sufficient attraction to sustain the relationship.

The second difficulty is that you will inevitably come across some-one who is more attractive than your partner. This is true no matter what feature attracted you most strongly in the first instance. This new attraction may just be a phase, and it may serve to confirm the relationship you are in; but a relationship based on attraction will always be vulnerable. It certainly needs to be present, but it is no basis for marriage.

I know my father loved my mother when he married her, but I am not sure whether he had thought things through. His commitment to the situation didn't really match the measure of his love. Soon after their wedding the marriage began to crumble. He spent most evenings away, leaving her alone to look after two sons, and she became quite bitter. Over two decades later, through much anger, agony and victimization of each other, they are still together; only waiting till my younger brother goes to university before they get divorced. I'm sure they still love each other somewhere deep down, but there is too much pain and fear to make up the difference. (Simon, 20)

private

The high divorce rate and poor experiences of family life have left many cynical about marriage. They argue that having a bit of paper does not make any real difference in the way people feel about each other. Commitment becomes a private transaction between two people. They alone understand the nature of this commitment and are not accountable to any other parties. When we have seen others fail, the temptation to try and work things out on personal terms is strong. But these private transactions are no better at delivering the lasting love we long for. The average length of time for which unmarried couples live together is under three years. The average length of a marriage in the UK in 1997 was between nine and ten years. Statistically, then, the private deals we strike fare significantly worse than the public vows we try to avoid. What we face is not just a crisis in marriage, but a crisis in commitment.

temporary

An actress in her early thirties was interviewed about her two 'failed marriages'. She took great offence at the assumption in the question. 'With one, we were together for two years,' she replied, 'and with the next for four. That's six happy years. You can't call that a failure.'

As we've just seen, relationships do not last the course. The pressures of modern life take their toll: financial problems, family difficulties, work-related stress all make marriage inconvenient at times. Our throwaway society teaches us that, when an item is not working, it is easier to dispose of it and get a new one than to get it repaired. This may be fine for a broken toaster, but people are worth more and deserve more. (That applies to the workplace too, where short-term contracts and redundancy do little to promote loyalty, stickability and faithfulness.)

The 'try before you buy' experiment has also failed to deliver longer-term security. One survey showed that couples who cohabit before marriage are about 40% more likely to have divorced within fifteen years of marriage than those who do not.

superficial

Marriage is often seen as sharing aspects of life, rather than as a union of the whole of life. Couples retain separate interests and circles of friends; increasing numbers of couples do not have joint bank accounts. Some make prenuptial agreements to determine the allocation of assets in the event of divorce. Many employers take little account of employees' family life, and couples can find themselves separated by work obligations for extended periods. Not all this is necessarily wrong, and couples seldom have full control over their circumstances; but such factors do serve to reinforce the superficial way in which many couples relate. Just surviving takes up so much time and effort that sex easily becomes their only experience of intimacy, and even that can fall into neglect.

Our society's ideas of marriage affect us all. Christians do not have a monopoly on happy marriages, nor are we immune to failure. I have been a guest at a number of weddings of Christian couples who are no longer together. As a society, we have thrown away God's ideas on marriage, relationships and family, leading to the disintegration of the family and the shredding of society. What needs to change is not just our practice, but our underlying attitude.

marriage as God intended

The LORD God said, 'It is not good for the man to be alone. I will make a helper suitable for him.'

Now the LORD God had formed out of the ground all the beasts of the field and all the birds of the air. He brought them to the man to see what he would name them, and whatever the man called each living creature, that was its name. So the man gave names to all the livestock, the birds of the air and all the beasts of the field.

But for Adam no suitable helper was found. So the LORD God caused the man to fall into a deep sleep; and while he was sleeping he took one of the man's ribs and closed up the place with

marriage and singleness

flesh. Then the LORD God made a woman from the rib he had taken out of the man, and he brought her to the man.

The man said,

> 'This is now bone of my bones
> and flesh of my flesh;
> she shall be called "woman",
> for she was taken out of man.'

For this reason a man will leave his father and mother and be united to his wife, and they will become one flesh.

The man and his wife were both naked, and they felt no shame.

(Genesis 2:18–25)

> A lot of people talk about marriage as give and take. We say emphatically that this is not true! Marriage is give and *receive*. To talk about taking sounds as if you have the right demand out of the relationship. But if you give, you can also receive. It is this sense of partnership that brings you closer together. (Shirley and Bill, married for forty years)

based on partnership

The husband and wife are made to complement each other. Suitability is more important than eligibility. We meet many people who are eligible to be our partner, but not all will be suitable. A key aspect of this first marriage, the marriage of Adam and Eve, is that God provides the partner. Many church marriage services still pay lip-service to this notion. 'Those whom God has joined together, man must not separate.' Yet God's involvement in the union is often neglected. We prefer to make the crucial decisions ourselves in our search for a partner. Sometimes we ask God to bless our decisions, but are not always willing to trust him. Clearly, there is a balance to be struck between trusting God to lead us to a partner and making the necessary effort to go out and meet people. The way forward in

121

a relationship may become clear only as we take it step by step, seeking God's best for our lives.

Sometimes we see a better model of partnership in business than in marriage: such a partnership is a legal agreement binding on the relevant parties, who become committed to work in the same business towards the same ends. Partnership means sharing the profits, yes, but the losses too.

public

According to the Genesis narrative, before a man and a woman come together, they leave their respective parents. This is an act of will and a public statement. If a marriage is to be successful, the bonds between husband and wife must be stronger even than bonds with parents or children. The public aspect of marriage is important; it enables a couple to take their place in a community where everybody understands the nature of their commitment to each other. This is more than a bit of paper. In many cultures, the public aspect of the couple's leaving their families and coming together is the basis of the marriage ceremony.

> Marriage is a partnership. But it is not just about a couple being together; it is about the wider Christian community. It is when people get alongside a couple that they can make a vital difference. We need marriages to grow and develop, and none of us can do this alone; we need the community to help. (David Cook)

permanent

The idea of the couple's being 'united' (Genesis 2:24) signifies being joined in such a way that separation is difficult. The union that God ordained was not temporary, but one that lasts for the whole of life. Its permanence is based not on feelings, but on promises, which are made publicly before witnesses and in the presence of God. When a marriage comes apart, both people are torn and damaged. Much of the damage may have been done before the actual separation or divorce, and, for some, separating may in fact be a grace and a mercy; but the hurt of the final severance should not be underestimated.

intimate

Genesis describes the intimacy of the couple's relationship as becoming 'one flesh'. This emphasis on bodily union underlines the fact that sexual intercourse is meant for marriage. The order of the events — leaving, being united and becoming one flesh — is important; relationships are public and permanent *before* they become sexual. Much of the Bible's teaching on sexual morality relates back to these important verses where the principle is established. (For instance, look up Matthew 19:3–9 on divorce; Ephesians 5:28–31 on prostitution; and Ephesians 5:28–31 on marriage.)

The 'one flesh' teaching also helps us appreciate that the marriage union is designed to be much more than sexual. It is a gift of God and a means of grace. In the lifelong union of marriage, we can know the joy of God, who made us in his own image, male and female. Marriage is founded on God's own loving nature and in the covenant of love he has established with those who are in Christ. Husband and wife, in giving themselves to each other in love, reflect the love of Christ for his church. In Christian marriage, husband and wife are called to live together faithfully, to love each other with respect, tenderness and delight. The companionship and comfort of marriage enable the full expression of physical love between husband and wife. Through their home life they help to shape a society in which human dignity and happiness may flourish and abound. God's plan is for an intimate relationship where, together, the couple become more than the individuals were on their own. Marriage is more than the sum of its parts. This growing relationship is characterized by sharing the whole of life (though Genesis talks about becoming one person, not spending all you time with one person!).

There are people who have gone through a marriage ceremony but do not follow the Maker's instructions for their marriage. Some celebrities seem to approach marriage in the same way as they buy their cars, constantly trading in their spouse for a new and sleeker model. They are married, but not as God intended. Other people never go through a marriage ceremony, but live together as husband and wife, own houses jointly, bring up children together, and are faithful to each other. Some of these relationships correspond more closely to marriage as God intended than some actual marriages do.

Marriage as God intended, however, is not simply a matter of public vows and permanent commitment to the 'one flesh' relationship. It is a matter of seeking God's help and power together throughout your life. God supplied the pattern for the relationship, but he also desires to be intimately involved in it. The writer of Ecclesiastes says, 'A cord of three strands not quickly broken' (4:12). This is true both in friendship and in marriage. The strength to live as God intends is not found inside ourselves. God alone can strengthen our fragile relationships.

12. singleness and marriage

I don't want to hand over my identity by taking someone else's name; I sometimes wake at night in a cold sweat at the idea of being Mrs Someone. I look at married couples and I don't think it looks like much fun to me. They're the ones who walk into parties and immediately head for opposite ends of the room. The wives complain that they never have sex anymore, the husbands complain that they are emasculated and misunderstood. We're told that marriage is hard work, a long emotional slog, not just a walk in the park. I've heard women say that they never knew what it was like to be really lonely until they got married.

Tania Kindersley

Single women outnumber marriageable men by 7.3 million in the United States. And most of the available ones are not in church. So unless we disobey God outright by marrying a non-Christian, let's face it: many of us will never marry. I have yet to hear this fact bluntly stated at any seminar I have ever attended. The thought of celibacy frightens us and we avoid it. Well-meaning friends tell us to believe God for a mate. But God doesn't promise us that we will ever marry. He promises us himself. But who is really teaching us how to know this God of immeasurable tenderness and gentleness who can help us, especially at night, when many lonely singles experience the 'claw down the walls' variety of sexual temptations?

Julia Duin

People have very different views of singleness. Some see it as a blessing, others as a curse. The word 'single' is not used in the Bible at all; its term is 'unmarried'. This might seem like semantics, but the idea of being single, in the sense of being on your own, is never what God intended for anybody. We are all designed to live in community. Part of the tragedy of modern western church life is that we often emphasize the nuclear family to the detriment of the church family. Many nuclear families in churches adopt an exclusive attitude to others in the church. Unmarried people are expected to form friendships only with others in the same situation, or may even be left on their own altogether.

It is not easy being single. Those around us may assume that we must be ugly, frigid or gay. Parents can accuse us of not trying hard enough to bring about the wedding and grandchildren they crave, and cannot understand what was wrong with that nice Mike or Susan. Social occasions that demand a partner can feel awkward. Weddings can turn into occasions to be dreaded, where you see yet another friend picked off, meet other friends with bouncing babies, and feel like the last single person on earth. It is easy to believe that all our troubles are caused by being single and to long for marriage as the answer to our difficulties.

Being unmarried, however, is not a second-rate option. Marriage and singleness are two alternative destinies, both of which are valid and are good for a Christian. In 1 Corinthians 7, Paul makes the point several times that it is good not to marry.

Are you unmarried? Do not look for a wife. But if you do marry, you have not sinned; and if a virgin marries, she has not sinned. But those who marry will face many troubles in this life, and I want to spare you this. (1 Corinthians 7:27–28)

Being unmarried is endorsed as good and entailing advantages. Those who are unmarried can concern themselves with the Lord's affairs and can serve and love God with an undivided heart (verses 32–35). Both being married and being unmarried have joys and privileges.

singleness as God intended

Marriage is the norm at present. The majority of us will get married and must take the associated responsibilities seriously. Yet singleness is not abnormal. Some wrongly see singleness as a choice for men and a sentence for women. Many godly, intelligent, articulate, gifted and attractive people do not get married. There are many reasons. Sometimes it is by choice, sometimes by circumstance, and sometimes by God's calling. Jesus chose not to get married, and was willing to live as a virgin, although he was tempted like us. 'We do not have a high priest who is unable to sympathize with our weaknesses, but we have one who has been tempted in every way, just as we are – yet was without sin' (Hebrews 4:15). Jesus was not a failure because he did not take a wife. His life was not a lonely existence, but was full of friendship and fruitfulness. He was not waiting for a woman. He was a fully functioning, fulfilled human being without a sexual partner. This should not be as surprising as it often seems in our society. Service, friendship, love and glory are found not only in romantic relationships, but also in faith, friendship, family and community. This may not always be our experience, but it was Jesus' experience and this should matter to us. To try to argue that it was OK for Jesus ('He was perfect and divine, but it's different for us') is to fail to appreciate that he was fully human.

There is a general myth that you are happier in a relationship than out of one; that you are more fulfilled with a partner. All of this is tied up with the expectations of others, that if you are in a relationship you will be having sex. Coming at these issues from a Christian perspective raises quite a few eyebrows and it is difficult to maintain integrity **❯** (Jonathan, 23)

it is not good to be alone

When God created Adam, he said, 'It is not good for the man to be alone' (Genesis 2:18). This is true for both married and single people. A scientific study of the American Medical Association in 1997 showed that loners were four times more likely to come down with a cold than people rich in relationships. Lack of social support does not just have dramatic health consequences; it also affects our emotional and spiritual well-being. We need to work at building a network of relationships in which we can both give and receive support. Sometimes we can spend so long focusing on the one relationship we do not have that we miss the tremendous opportunities that are on our doorstep. Singleness does afford opportunities to develop quality friendships with other people. Many single people appreciate this, though it can be a struggle to get the message through to their married friends!

❮ The media bombard us with images that tell us we have to find our identity in someone else. This is especially true of the student world, where you are not really someone without someone else. All of this is unhelpful when you are trying to figure out who you actually are. This is where Jesus makes a radical difference. I know that he likes and loves me for who I am, and so it doesn't really matter what others say and think about me. My identity is in Jesus. **❯** (Becca, 23)

we can serve God

All of us can use our gifts for God. This again is true for both married and single people. It is a fallacy to believe that the key to effective growth lies in our marital status. We will not necessarily be more effective because we are married or because we are single. Our circumstances will be important in determining how and where we serve. All Christians have opportunities to serve which will vary throughout their lives. The important thing is to be using the gifts that God has given us in the place where he has put us. There are no second-class citizens in the kingdom of God. We all have opportunities to invest meaningfully in other people. Both married and single people can love and care. The growth of the church through history has been advanced by married and unmarried, men and women, young and old from every culture and stratum of society. We should not make the mistake of imagining that we could serve more effectively if we were married or if we were single. Rather, we should look to encourage each other to the best of our abilities.

sexual purity is precious

The attitudes of those around us can grind us down over time. We begin to wonder why we have bothered waiting all these years. Sex is so much seen as a basic human right, essential to human fulfilment, that living without it seems impossible. The same God who made us sexual beings has a stake in our sexual purity and has given us the capacity to please him in the way we handle our sexuality. We do, however, need help to work out appropriate ways of expressing and receiving affirmation and love. Being unmarried does not make you untouchable, but the appropriate use of touch is not always an easy balance to strike.

live for today

You do not know how long you will be single, and you probably don't need to decide that now. It is difficult to be always wondering when you will meet the right person, but it is also difficult to live with the assumption that you will never get married. Questions about the future can paralyse us in the present, and we need to make sure we don't let that happen.

The life skills you learn as a single person will be valuable whatever the future holds. Involving other people in making decisions about your career, car, family, housing and holidays will help you make better choices. This approach will prove useful if you do get married, and doubly useful if you do not!

Do not dwell on what you have not got. Rather, be thankful for the many blessings you do have, and make the most of them. Today is a unique opportunity; it will not occur again.

looking for a partner?

Marriage is not something to enter into because we feel empty on our own, and expect marriage somehow to fill the vacuum. A good marriage is not founded on falling in love, a job, or material goods, but on something much more solid. God has given us all we need to live the way he wants us to. Marriage will not deliver the perfection, intimacy and rescue we crave.

Single people must ask themselves why they want to get married. It should be clear that the need for emotional compensation, the urgency of escaping from a troubled and unhappy home, the lostness created by our environment, and even good, legitimate reasons like 'being in love' are not good reasons on their own. Here are some questions it is worth asking about any potential partner.

- Is this person of the opposite sex?
- Is this person a Christian?
- Is this person making a difference where God has placed him or her now?
- Do you feel God leading you both in the same general direction?
- What factors would make this person a suitable (or unsuitable) partner for you?
- What would make this person a good (or bad) parent to your children, should you have them?
- What do your friends think of this person?
- What do you like (or dislike) about the way this person interacts with his or her own parents and with yours?
- Have you discussed everyday matters, like home and money, and what do you agree (or disagree) on?
- Do you love this person for himself or herself more than for what he or she gives you?

But get a life! There are important issues to fill your horizon with. We must recognize the special gift and calling we have *now*, whether married or single. We must have a sense of urgency, making the best use of our time and opportunities because the days are short. Relationships can either serve or hinder that calling.

opportunities in marriage and singleness

The same basic challenges face us all as Christians, regardless of our marital status. Both married and single people are called to live revolutionary lives and enjoy relationships on a new plane; to model patterns of behaviour which go beyond the mediocrity of the world, and set the agenda for our families, communities and societies.

This radical difference must be lived out in the details of life. Married and unmarried people can help each other to fulfil the daily calling that God gives to us all. This will happen best when we try to understand each other's lives. Married couples easily imagine that single people have nothing valuable to contribute to their situation, and *vice versa*.

I firmly believe that the best place to work out these issues is in the context of the local church. Your own local church may be far from the ideal community, but I doubt there is anything else like it in your neighbourhood. Where else can young and old, male and female, married and unmarried come together to share each others' lives? The local church, when it works as it should, is one of the few places where people can experience true community in the modern world. It should be a place where people worship and learn together, where truth is proclaimed, where the weak are assisted, the lonely welcomed and those on the margins of society included.

These are great ideas, but we move towards the ideal only when each of us is committed to being part of the solution and not part of the problem. There are several practical steps we could take:

— Do you see your home as a place to exercise the gift of hospitality? Do you have people round for meals or to stay?

- Do you see your friendships as opportunities to bring in new people? Does your circle of friends include people in a variety of circumstances?
- Do you see special occasions as opportunities to widen your circle of friends?
- Do you see the task of bringing up children as a church responsibility? Other couples and single people can share in the joys and responsibilities of parenthood, helping the children grow and develop.
- Are you interested in the work that other people are doing, and in the encouragements and stresses they face?
- Do you pray for other people's growth and service?
- Do you support people as they care for relatives or friends who are ill, elderly or disabled?
- Do you consider how you can be a gift to others by freeing up time for them, giving them a break or helping them in some practical way?

I am still learning to live like this. What little I know has been taught by many committed friends over the years. We as a family could not function as we do without the care and input of married and single friends. They invite us for meals, put us up when we are travelling, look after the children, lend us cars, care for us in practical ways, pray for us regularly and enrich our lives with their love.

Don't let your marriage or your singleness be a barrier to service or love. Look for the unique opportunities you have to invest in those around you. How can God use your particular situation to make you a blessing to others?

homosexuality

13. homosexuality

The New Queer Politics looks beyond equality and challenges the assumption that lesbian and gay desire is an intrinsically minority sexual orientation. It argues that everyone is potentially homosexual (and heterosexual). While some biological factors may predispose individuals to a sexual preference, all the psychological and anthropological evidence suggests that sexuality is primarily culturally conditioned, and is not rigidly compartmentalised. None of us is wholly attracted to one sex or the other. We are all a mixture of desires. Some we express, others we repress.

Peter Tatchell, *The Independent*, 26 July 1992

what does God think of homosexuals?

God's attitude towards homosexuals is not in doubt. God loves homosexuals. God loves all people equally. God's love is not conditional upon race, gender, age, class, or sexual orientation. God loved 'the world' so much that he sent his Son, Jesus, who died on the cross for that whole world. His offer of life is extended to all who believe, without condition. Nobody is excluded from God's love and his rescuing work.

I do not believe that God divides people on the basis of their sexual orientation. I see no evidence of discrimination in the Bible, and do not think that God puts people into such categories as lesbian, gay, bisexual and heterosexual. Our identity as human beings is not primarily shaped by our sexual orientation or preference, but by our creation in the image of God. His image is broken in all of us, and in that lies the cause of all of our frustration, heartache, prejudice and pain. Many people perceive their primary need to be sexual, whereas in reality it is spiritual.

It is a tragedy that the church has not always communicated this clearly. Far too frequently through its history, people grappling with their sexual identity have been marginalized and condemned. At times, the church has spoken more vociferously against homosexuality than against other sexual sins and practices. Seldom have churches felt like safe places where issues of sexual identity can be considered and explored with compassion. Rather, the church has tended to impose a uniform grid, which does not fit with the individual's experience. People have been processed rather than respected as individuals, and have not been helped to find the best way forward for them. (It is particularly ironic that the gay community has not always been the best place for people to work through issues of sexual identity for precisely the same reasons.) As a Christian, I am willing to shoulder some responsibility for the inadequate response that we have extended to many people.

The church is not alone in misunderstanding homosexual people. Society is also to blame. The treatment of professing gay and lesbian people over generations has been shameful, and has served only to create and entrench the gay ghetto.

the search for identity

People are all unique individuals and must be treated as such. Sexual orientation covers a wide spectrum, from those who would describe themselves as entirely heterosexual, to those who would describe themselves as entirely homosexual, with many shades in between. Many people also move across this spectrum in one direction or the other, through the course of their lives. To attempt to dismiss, resolve or categorize individuals in a brief encounter is to oversimplify a complex issue.

Some have sought to identify the cause of homosexuality, seeking to pin it down to genetics, environment or choice. But it is not possible to consider the reasons for homosexual orientation apart from a wider understanding of the struggles we all face in our search for identity. In that search, our genetic make-up, family background, environment and experiences all have their influence. In each of us, these elements combine in different ways. All of us are born into a broken world and daily experience the reality of those imperfections within and around us. The search for identity is at the core of our humanity. It is not a gay issue, but a human issue. I am opposed to anything that puts people's sexuality higher up the agenda than their humanity.

We have seen that the Bible teaches that God created us with an inbuilt need for intimacy. This is to be experienced first and foremost with God himself, but there is also a legitimate need for intimacy with others – the kind where the real me meets the real you. Sexual intercourse was designed to play only a minor part in that intimacy within a monogamous, lifelong, committed marriage relationship. We know that the world does not function now as God intended. We have seen that it is fractured at its most fundamental level. That fracture affects every part of human psychology, biology and sociology. The fact that things are wrong in our sexuality is a symptom of what is wrong with humanity. Issues of the heart cannot be resolved in sexual activity or experimentation.

The identity that God wants to give us in Christ does not fit naturally with any of us. God wants to make us his friends; by nature we are all his enemies. God wants us to live in the light; by nature we prefer darkness. God wants to give us eternal life; by nature we are all dying. This is stark language, but the contrasts are starkly drawn throughout the Bible. The desires, thoughts and attitudes that lie at the heart of the human condition are completely at odds with the direction God intends for us.

For everyone, without exception, becoming a Christian involves a radical change of orientation. We no longer live by our natural feelings and desires, but rather live in Christ. We begin to find our identity in Christ when we receive life in his name. The first verse I ever memorized as a Christian underlines this: 'I have been crucified with Christ and I no longer live, but Christ lives in me. The life I live in the body, I live by faith in the Son of God, who loved me and gave himself for me' (Galatians 2:20).

Life in all its fullness is available to us all. Identity is found not in sexuality, but in Jesus Christ alone.

We discover our lives and identities not in our natural selves, but in Christ. Our natural selves must become less influential and their power over us must diminish. This is not to deny who we are, but to discover our true identity and destiny. In Christ we do not become clones or stereotypes. In Christ we become the unique individuals that we were each created to be.

These general points have particular implications for those who have a high sense of their homosexual orientation. Behaviour can feel natural and right, and yet seem to clash with what God says in his Word. This can cause considerable hurt and confusion. We need to grasp the truth that what comes naturally is not necessarily right. Far from it! The battle against our natural desires is an unavoidable part of the struggle for all of us. The focus of the battle will be different for each of us, but the underlying issue is the same. If you are struggling with your natural identity, you are not alone. We all face this struggle.

God's primary desire is not that we should become heterosexual, but that we should become more like Christ. This is not something any of us can resolve on our own. Our true destiny can be discovered only within the Christian community. This is true for everyone, regardless of their orientation. Other communities offer a sense of identity and destiny; that is one of the main attractions of joining a group. Once we have enjoyed a particular experience, we tend to join with others who enjoy it too. Almost before we know it, we have adopted the mannerisms and dress associated with the group identity, and find our friends exclusively in the group. We allow our identity and destiny to be shaped by the norms of the group to which we belong and the way society categorizes us. This can be true of all sorts of groups, and is often true of the gay community. People have an experience and are encouraged to interpret it within a particular conceptual framework. Whatever community we belong to, we must be willing to challenge its norms and consider how they relate to the truth.

what the Bible says about homosexuality

We ought not to try to consider what the Bible says on any specific matter without reference to the wider issue of which it forms a part. The Bible is primarily concerned not with sexual behaviour, but with God's plan to rescue a people who will love him eternally. Homosexuality is mentioned seven times in the Old and New Testaments. These verses have not always been handled with integrity by Christian teachers.

The judgment on Sodom and Gomorrah in Genesis 19 has more to do with general immorality, violence and lack of hospitality (a major failing in that culture) than with homosexuality alone.

In Leviticus, there are two regulations concerning homosexual acts. One (18:22) prohibits a man from lying with a man in the same way as a woman. The sentence here is awkward, because there is no technical term for 'homosexuality' in the Hebrew. Nevertheless, it is a clear general prohibition of male homosexual behaviour. The fact that lesbian behaviour is not mentioned does not diminish the impact of the verse. The penalty for male homosexual acts is given in Leviticus 20:13 as death. Male homosexual behaviour is one of several crimes this chapter lists as deserving this punishment, and is not singled out for special attention. These two verses are the sum total of the legal comments about homosexuality in the Hebrew Bible. They are important to note, but must also be considered in context.

The New Testament references to homosexuality are largely in Paul's writing. In Romans 1:26–27, lesbian sex and homosexual sex are described as marks of shameful lust and perversion. I Corinthians 6:9 lists 'homosexual offenders' as among the unrighteous who will not inherit the kingdom of God. These are difficult verses and, again must be considered in context.

I believe the Bible is unambiguous in its prohibition of homosexual activity. This case does not depend on a few verses, but rests on the whole biblical understanding of sex and sexuality. It is clear that the only kind of sexual relationship that God intends and permits is between one man and one woman in marriage. This is why homosexual relationships are not acceptable. They are not what God intended from the beginning, not what he delights in now, and not a part of the new community that he is creating, which will last for ever. This is just as true of heterosexual sex that takes place outside marriage.

I know its seems an appalling affront to human sensibilities, but God has placed clear limits on the use and enjoyment of sex. God has placed restrictions on everybody's sexual activity. Premarital sex, extramarital sex and homosexual sex are all condemned as not being God's best for humankind. This seems particularly harsh if you are conscious of a strong homosexual orientation. I want to emphasize again that there are no contradictions in God's love, and that his love for you is real.

pointers for those who are struggling

People who have not experienced homosexual desires find it hard to understand the depth of pain and confusion felt by men and women who have. What follows has been gleaned from the personal experience of Christians who have lived through, and still live with, the struggle.

recognize who you are

God does not see us as gay, lesbian, bisexual or straight. He sees us as either in or out of relationship with himself. Getting our relationship with God sorted out is of primary importance. Our identity is in Christ, not in our sexuality or our struggle. We are not powerless to make choices when faced with sexual preferences, or doomed to remain the same for ever. We must never lose sight of God's willingness to accept us as we are and to draw close to us.

At the age of twelve or thirteen I realized with a huge shock that I was sexually attracted to the same sex, that I was one of 'them', that I was a poof. I was often called that name at school; little did they know it was the truth. There was no-one I felt I could tell. I was a Christian even at that age, but there wasn't anyone in the church I was close enough to to share with. I couldn't bring myself to tell my family. I didn't want to hurt or disappoint them. So I kept it to myself – my little secret.

I would frequently become depressed, desiring only to be normal, feeling such shame, guilt and loneliness. Sometimes I would cry myself to sleep at night. At these times Jesus was the only one who was there for me; only he knew. Sometimes I would look in the mirror and say. 'I hate you.' I couldn't accept who I was.

I made a few really good friends at university. They were the first people who really seemed to like me. It was great to feel wanted, to know that other people actually wanted me around. This gave me some confidence in myself and raised my self-esteem a little. Gradually I became less convinced that I was the jerk and geek that I had always been called at school.

It was during this time, after ten long years of struggle, loneliness, secrecy and depression, that I sought help, fearing that I might give up the struggle with homosexuality and start to embrace and express it. Through the wisdom of some Christian counsellors, God met my pain and hurt. I was able to look at the issue from his perspective and see myself for who I was, as his son, rather than the person I thought I was in my failure and brokenness. I saw how much God cared for me and loved me, how he had never left me, and how he was with me even in my loneliest moments. He was

the relationships revolution

there to help me with my struggle, not condemning me for who I was.

I am still struggling with my sexuality, but I try to see myself no longer in terms of sexual identity, but in terms of my identity in Christ. ❯ (Steve, 23)

you are not alone

Lots of people struggle with the same issues as you. Do not be tempted to isolate yourself. There are people you can talk to. You are not alone in your situation, but the more you consider yourself to be alone, the harder it will become. Try to develop friendships where you can talk openly and honestly about your failures and victories to people who will keep loving, supporting and challenging you, whom you can trust, and with whom you can feel safe. A Christian family can be a special haven, though this may require some work on your part, especially if your church does not organize links between singles and families.

❮ I grew up with a sense of being 'different'. I engaged in sexual activity from an early age, and was holding out for the perfect partner, the man who would meet the aching inside for love and affirmation. I became a Christian at seventeen. For two years I had only the most rudimentary understanding of what it meant; it made no great impact on my life.

Then, at nineteen, I met Robert, a man who fulfilled all my criteria, and got into a relationship with him. The intimacy was great. He loved me, and I him. But after the initial joys, a deep dissatisfaction settled in. How could this man satisfy the deepest inner longings of another human being? It was too much to expect of anyone – anyone but God. I soon saw that an ongoing relationship with Robert was at odds with the relationship I had with Jesus.

At that point, I was not quite sure why, but I knew it was wrong. I chose Jesus: not an easy choice, or one that felt good at the time. But I knew that all I had hoped for in Robert – the intimacy, love, freedom and security that I had found briefly through sex and rela-

140

tionships – could be delivered in a full and lasting way only in relationship with God through Jesus❯ (Andy, 26)

be realistic about change

Of course we want to have arrived and to have put our struggles behind us. Do not be tempted to paper over the cracks and pretend that unresolved issues are dealt with. Change will not happen overnight. It may not happen in the way you expect or hope, and will not be painless. But it is better to persevere than to give in, and it is possible to live with integrity and discover reality. Your progress may be 'a day at a time'. Failure along the way does not signify that there is no more hope of change or growth. There are no easy answers or quick-fix solutions, but God's grace is sufficient, his love is real and his power is made perfect in weakness. Others have walked this road before.

be aware of your limitations

Be careful. Do not put yourself in the way of temptation. There may be films it is better not to watch, magazines it is better not to read and social contexts it is better to avoid.

Things started to change quite subtly – a touch here, a gentle back-rub there, a shoulder-massage – all very innocent yet compelling. The inevitable happened a few weeks later. It all felt right and natural. All common sense left me. I didn't care who hurt me after that. She was everything. Right things were wrong. Wrong things felt right. I was completely engulfed, consumed even, and if God hadn't intervened I don't know where I would be now. If I was a young teenager, maybe I would have believed or convinced myself that I was a lesbian, even though I had never had any such feelings for a woman before her or even after her.

She moved away. I was bereft. It took months to get over her, but God was faithful. In those months, I still felt bound in chains to her and to my feelings. Yet gently the restraints were broken. For me, Psalm 107 spoke loudly and still reminds me to this day what God did:

> Some sat in darkness, dark as death,
>   prisoners bound fast in iron,
> because they had rebelled against God's commands
>   and flouted the purpose of the Most High.
> Their spirit subdued by hard labour;
>   they stumbled and fell with none to help them.
> So they cried to the LORD in their trouble,
>   and he saved them from their distress;
> he brought them out of darkness, dark as death,
>   and broke their chains.

I knew God had broken the chains that had held me fast. I threw away all the letters she had written me and all the other gifts and stuff we'd shared, and I begged forgiveness for all the hurt I had caused other people due to this relationship. I am careful now of a friendship where it always seems to be just the two of you. Things get distorted very gradually; you don't realize what is happening — and suddenly the caring and sharing become an obsession. **❯**
(Mary, 35)

relating to gay people

For a variety of reasons, there can be tensions in establishing good friendships with those whose sexual orientation differs from our own. The following is not intended to patronize, but to offer common-sense, practical advice on dealing with some of these tensions.

treat each other with love and respect

Relating to people of different sexual orientations should be no different from relating to anybody else, yet it can become complex because of our own prejudices and insecurities. Our approach in friendship with people who call themselves gay, lesbian or bisexual should not be determined by their sexual behaviour. We are all broken people, and in that respect there is no 'them and us'.

speak the truth

We need to speak the truth (see Ephesians 4:15) correctly, clearly, consistently and compassionately. We must acknowledge that we are all being addressed by this same truth and are vulnerable to inappropriate thoughts, feelings and behaviour. We speak the truth not as though we were sinless, but as sinners in whom God has begun a good work. We should not avoid answering questions about God's standards of sexual morality.

For some people, the cost of following Jesus will be most evident in this area of their lives, and we must take care not to diminish the cost of responding to the gospel's challenge.

don't be afraid

We should not let homophobic myths influence our behaviour. We can be encouraged to believe that God hates homosexuals, that all gay men are camp, that all lesbians are butch and that bisexuals are greedy. This stereotyping can even lead us to worry that we might be a potential target for friends with a different orientation. We should not flatter ourselves! We shall be no more attractive to the majority of homosexual people than to the majority of heterosexual ones. There is more than one dimension to people who struggle with their sexual orientation. Don't be afraid to talk and ask questions, and don't shy away from close friendships isolating them.

set an example

Lots of people in our society don't relate to gay and lesbian people for fear of contamination. They worry that they will be infected by their ideas; or that by associating with them they will get labelled gay or lesbian too, and be ridiculed by their friends and colleagues. As Christians, we must not let the world set the agenda for our relationships. Jesus associated with outcasts. He assisted the weak and befriended the lonely. He was often accused by the religious hierarchy of being a friend of sinners, and was willing to defy the social conventions of his day. He touched those regarded as untouchable and loved those considered unlovable. In following this pattern, our goal is not primarily to change people's behaviour, but to introduce them to Jesus. He alone can change our hearts and transform our lives. He will tackle issues of sexuality at the appropriate time.

being **R**evolutionary

14. being a revolutionary

Under the many oppressive systems of government this world has endured, ordinary people have felt marginalized and dictated to. Their capacity to choose has been undermined. In such situations, people of good conscience are faced with a stark challenge. Do you tacitly endorse the system, or do you work for drastic change? Being a revolutionary is not an easy option, but it is the only viable alternative to endorsing the system. Real revolutionaries are willing to put their lives on the line for a principle, idea or person, in the hope that things could and should be better.

The history of the church is the story of a revolution, starting with a small group of ordinary people, and turning the world upside down. Christians should be the most radical people on the planet! Today, society desperately needs revolutionaries who will take a stand against its norms, who will sacrifice all in the service of their Lord and of the people around them. The cost of the battle is great; hardship is unavoidable. Yet when people's eternal destiny is at stake, to remain silent is betrayal. To walk the path of indifference or self-satisfaction is not to follow in the footsteps of Christ. Dare to be different! Take a stand! Join the revolution!

I have been challenged by the lives of many young people who have sought to be part of God's revolution. Yet I am constantly amazed at their surprise on encountering struggles and problems. Experiencing trouble does not always indicate that you are doing something wrong. It may well indicate that you are getting nearer the front-line. Because of our union with Christ, we are involved in a spiritual conflict raging in the heavenly realms.

One of the most strategic battlegrounds in this conflict is that of relationships and sexuality. The battle rages not just around us, but within us. We should not be surprised by this battle, or by the temptations and difficulties it creates. We are fighting from a position of victory; Satan was defeated at the cross and will be finally overthrown when Christ returns. But in the meantime we are still faced by an opponent who hates us and will do all he can to deceive and hurt us.

People sometimes become resentful about their sexuality. They argue that if it causes so much hassle we would be better off without it. But learning how to deal with it and express it is part of our spiritual battle. The battle gets fierce, and at times threatens to overwhelm us, but the union with Christ that draws us into the conflict also gives us hope and power and strength. Following Jesus means that we no longer indulge our natural desires and feelings, but live to please him. We deny ourselves, take up our cross daily, and follow him. We depend on God's grace.

The difference that Jesus makes is not that we are instantly changed, but that God has started a good work in us (Philippians 1:6). God has made us his friends and his children, but we are not yet all that we shall be. We need to tell ourselves the gospel, every day of our lives. At the heart of our being we are depraved and corrupt and opposed to God's work in us. God was fully aware of this when Christ died for us. It was precisely *why* Christ died for us! This is not always easy for us to take on board. We want to be accepted on our own merit and are frustrated that this can never be the case. We would like to feel that we have arrived, or at least that we are able to make progress on our own.

being a revolutionary

The more we appreciate who we are, the more we shall value what God has done for us in Christ, and the way he is transforming us.

A real person, Christ here and now, in that very room where you are saying your prayers, is doing things to you, interfering with your very self, killing the old natural self in you and replacing it with the kind of self he has ... turning you permanently into a different sort of thing, into a new little Christ, a being which in its own small way has the same kind of life as God, which shares in his power, joy, knowledge and eternity. (C. S. Lewis)

In the confession of concrete sins, the 'old man' dies a painful death before the eyes of another. Because this humiliation is so hard, we continue to scheme to evade confessing. (Dietrich Bonhoeffer)

Sometimes it feels impossible to cope. The stimulus of sights around us stirs up desires within us. These make us look and long for what is on offer around us. At times our hormones go into overdrive, and it seems like we could explode. But if we do not learn to control our sexuality, our sexuality will control us. Whatever we choose to worship will determine the people we become. The more we put sex first, the more sensual we become, and the less self-controlled and loving we become, and the less we think about what we are doing. The more we follow God's will, the more we please him and the more we demonstrate the difference that Christ makes. 'It is God's will ... that each of you should learn to control his own body in a way that is holy and honourable, not in passionate lust like the heathen, who do not know God' (1 Thessalonians 4:3–4).

We are not alone in the battle. The one who started our faith has promised to perfect it. This perfection will ultimately embrace the whole of our being, including our sexuality.

practical tips for revolutionaries

face up to the issues

Issues of sex and sexuality must be faced up to and resolved. We cannot pretend they are not there. Far too often we struggle on, feeling that we are on our own, that nobody else understands. We try to convince ourselves that we have resolved these issues, but know otherwise in our heart of hearts. The widening gulf between the person we are and the person we would like to be is bound to lead to disaster. Do not be tempted to ignore difficulties in the hope that they will go away. God promises to help us in this battle, but he wants us to participate. In learning to judge ourselves, in setting our minds on things above, in being transformed through the renewing of our minds, we become more like Christ (see I Corinthians 11:31; Colossians 3:1–3; Romans 12:2).

flee temptation and resist the devil

The Bible tells us to flee the evil desires of youth (2 Timothy 2:22), and to resist the devil and he will flee from us (James 4:7; see also I Peter 5:9). We make a major mistake when we try to do the reverse of what the Bible advocates; when, instead of fleeing temptation and resisting the devil, we try to resist temptation and flee the devil. Some temptations are virtually impossible to resist. The solution is to get out of the tempting environment. Trying to flee the devil is equally impossible. He prowls around like a roaring lion (I Peter 5:8).

When Joseph found himself the object of an attempted seduction by his master's wife, it was not appropriate for him to pray for help in resisting temptation. The only course of action open to him if he wanted to avoid sin was to flee the situation. He ran away, leaving his cloak behind. His action was misrepresented, and he lost his job and was imprisoned, but he maintained his integrity. The story is a good model for us. (Read it in Genesis 39.)

Sometimes people ask me how far they should go in a relationship. One answer I give is that it is wise to avoid any situation that makes fleeing difficult. I therefore think it is better for a couple not to undress each other. (It would be embarrassing to flee down the street with your clothes flapping behind you. Imagine meeting a friend, who asks, 'What are you doing in such a dishevelled state?' You reply, 'Fleeing temptation.' Your friend may well wonder if you should not have thought of that before.)

Secondly, I would avoid lying down together. When we are lying down, it is difficult to flee.

Thirdly, I would avoid turning each other on sexually. I believe we know when we are doing this, and when this is being done to us. When we are turned on, we do not want to flee, and probably cannot resist.

Fleeing temptation does not mean making a token effort and then coming back for more. It means getting out of the situation completely.

be careful what you fill your mind with

We reap what we sow (Galatians 6:7). What you put into your life has an effect. What you think about and value, and incorporate into your being, will in large measure determine the person you become. So we need to watch what we think about, and think about what we watch. We can find ourselves thinking about all sorts of things that don't benefit us, and not thinking about things that do. A colleague once told me, 'You know, you should really spend more time looking at paintings and sculpture and surveying the landscape of God's creation.' I thought he was crazy! On reflection, I realized that I did spend a lot of time watching and thinking about things that were not very beneficial. 'Whatever is true, whatever is noble, whatever is right, whatever is pure, whatever is lovely, whatever is admirable – if anything is excellent or praiseworthy – think about such things' (Philippians 4:8).

Television is a strange medium. Often we watch it for relaxation. It requires little brain-power, and we sit in front of it uncritically. We quickly take in all kinds of values and images which not only provide fuel for our fantasies, but influence the way in which we live. If something unhelpful comes on while a parent or friend is in the room, we will switch channels; but we are much slower to respond when we are on our own.

I live in a flat with three other lads. Every Saturday night we used to get a video out. There was nothing particularly pornographic about it; we were just getting 15s and 18s and enjoying a takeaway together. Eventually I began to realize that many of the scenes in the movies were not doing me any good at all. After two weeks of agonizing, I confronted the other guys and told them how I felt. To my surprise, some of them had been feeling the same. Together, we took the decision to get rid of the television. Since then, the quality of conversation and care in the flat has increased considerably. I am so glad we had the guts to take a stand. (Matthew, 22)

Large numbers of magazines, websites, phone lines, books and satellite channels offer sexually explicit material, covering sexual technique, statistical analysis of sex surveys, reports of sexual behaviour, descriptions of sexual activity and pictures of naked people. Their easy availability poses a particular problem for some. We thirst for knowledge. But our curiosity is corrupted and misdirected. Why do we desire to look at naked bodies? Why do we hunger to know details of people's sexual experiences? Why do we thirst for information on sexual technique?

Much of this information, which promises to enhance our lives and relationships, actually devalues them. Sexuality cannot be satisfying on celluloid, paper or screen. Whenever sexuality is removed from an interpersonal emotional context, it becomes less than God designed it to be. The effect of using such material is to make us less than God intends us to be. We easily fall into compulsive behaviour. Pornography becomes increasingly addictive and yet ever less satisfying. The buzz and excitement become increasingly hard to reproduce, and we may find ourselves locked into a pattern of fantasy and habitual masturbation.

If you are in such a situation, it is vital to make a clean break from whatever it is you are using. This may well involve financial cost and personal inconvenience. You may have a video collection that needs to be destroyed, magazines to be disposed of or disks to erase. You must be ruthless in this process. Do not be tempted to keep even your most precious magazine or picture. You will need the help of one or two friends you can trust in this. It may be best, in the short term, to get rid of your video recorder or your internet browser.

Addiction to sexually explicit material, like any addiction, is not easily broken. After a period of self-denial, it is tempting to imagine that you now deserve a treat. The more deeply you have been involved, the greater the struggle will be. But there is hope. You must be committed to long-term obedience in this matter.

Christians are not required to opt out of life in modern society. We can appreciate and understand what is going on without justifying or engaging in behaviour that does us no good.

get rid of sexual immorality

The Bible is clear on the attitude we should take to sexual immorality. Its language is harsh. We are to avoid sexual immorality and flee from it (1 Thessalonians 4:3; 1 Corinthians 6:18); indeed, we are to put it to death (Colossians 3:5). Many of us, far from trying to avoid it or flee from it, adopt a policy of peaceful co-existence. But if we do not put it to death, it will enslave us. Some of us are willing to kill it, but only gradually. We are like someone who kills himself by smoking; the method is effective in the end, but we want to enjoy it in the meantime. In the Bible, the way to put things to death is always with the sword of the Spirit, the Word of God (Ephesians 6:17). Being a double-edged sword (Hebrews 4:12), it cuts both ways. We need to use it on ourselves, getting rid of what should not be there. The sword of the Spirit is also the Word of life. Destroying our wrong thoughts and habits brings life and fruit to our beings.

learn to recognize danger

I once worked in a paper mill. The fork-lift truck drivers who worked there had to undergo safety training. This included watching a video which encouraged the drivers to identify potential dangers, 'paint them red' in their minds, and steer away from the hazard. Piles of crates, or the edge of a loading bay, would flash red on the video. The intention was to save lives by enabling the drivers to spot the danger-points where carelessness could cause accidents.

I recognize that there are thoughts, feelings and situations that I need to paint red because they could lead me into temptation. Similarly, there are particular hazards for you. It is important that you begin to recognize these and take evasive action. Jesus said, 'If your right eye causes you to sin, gouge it out and throw it away … And if your right hand causes you to sin, cut if off and throw it away' (Matthew 5:29). He was not advocating self-mutilation, but underlining the seriousness of sin and urging us to be ruthless in ridding ourselves of anything that would lead us into it. There are places it is better not to go, and circumstances in which we should be particularly careful.

Not all sexual behaviour takes place in the context of relationships. Sometimes a friendship can get out of hand. Sometimes people go and deliberately pick someone up with the intention of having a sexual encounter. This is entirely inappropriate for a Christian. It separates sex not only from marriage, but also from intimacy. To imagine that such behaviour does not have a price tag is plain stupid. Be very careful not to be alone with anyone in situations where this might tempt you.

Here are some danger-points to paint red in your mind:

- spending too much time alone with somebody
- watching television late at night
- anyone who tries to persuade you to do something against your will
- situations where you are conscious of sexual tension
- times when your body clock makes you more vulnerable
- not having anyone to talk to or pray with
- being away from home due to study, work or holidays
- feeling down or sad or lonely

being a revolutionary

The key is getting to know your own weaknesses and learning to live with a safety margin. This frees you to enjoy life as you explore within the boundary fence.

I was on the Christian Union committee and involved in a house group at church. When I was in these situations, everything was fine. But when I went out drinking with guys from the rugby club, things started to go wrong. I would often pick up a girl at a party or in a club and go back to her flat. I kept vowing it wouldn't happen again, but it did. My life seemed increasingly divided into two parts – a Christian part which was going fine, and a rugby part which was a complete nightmare. It was only when someone in the CU spoke to me about it that I felt challenged to face up to the situation. He was able to give me some help and point me in the right direction. (Mark, 23)

don't bring the gospel into disrepute

The standards God sets us are high. Even situations you could cope with, and which are not necessarily wrong, should be avoided if there is any danger of misunderstanding and dishonour to the name of Christ. The reputation of the gospel is at stake. Christians are members of Christ, and our bodies are not meant for sexual immorality (which harms both spirit and body), but for the Lord (1 Corinthians 6:13). We are meant to be his witnesses in the world, and to enjoy an intimate relationship with him. Appreciating all this motivates us, not to live legalistically, but to offer our bodies as living sacrifices (Romans 12:1).

use your freedom wisely

The Christians at Corinth had got hold of the idea of Christian freedom in a big way. 'Everything is permissible for me' was their slogan. Paul responds to this with a 'Yes, but'. Not everything is beneficial or constructive, he says. And some behaviour we indulge in can end up enslaving us. Where will our freedom be then? Instead of self-indulgence, he urges us to seek the good of others. (See 1 Corinthians 6:12; 10:23–24.)

We ought to use our freedom responsibly, avoiding behaviour that would lead us into slavery or our brother or sister into sin. Positively, we should choose behaviour that glorifies God. These principles give us a helpful checklist against which any behaviour can be evaluated. I find it particularly useful in considering issues of sexuality.

Is this behaviour leading me into slavery? Is it becoming a habit? Is it something I cannot live without, a desire that must be satisfied? Is it starting to control me?

Is it leading my brothers and sisters into sin? Is it helping them, or damaging them? There is no such thing as morally neutral behaviour. All our actions have either positive or negative results. Writing to the Corinthians, Paul deals with the question of whether Christians may eat meat that was offered to an idol before going on sale. Idols are nothing, he says, so it makes no difference to us whether we eat such meat or not. But it may well matter to others, for whom idols are still significant. They do not have the same capacity as we do, and we must respect their consciences. If we ate the meat in their presence, would we lead them into sin, and seem to compromise our Christian testimony? If our behaviour is likely to produce such results as these, we must be willing to stop it. (See 1 Corinthians 8:1–13; 10:25–33.)

Does it glorify God? Is God pleased and honoured by this behaviour? Is he happy that I am doing this? If other people knew that this was going on, would they give thanks to God because of it or would they be ashamed? We are called to be free – not free to indulge our sinful nature, but free to serve one another in love (Galatians 5:13). Society often promises freedom, but what is on offer is actually slavery. You are free only within certain parameters. Jesus says, 'If the Son sets you free, you will be free indeed' (John 8:36). He alone offers true freedom.

discipline your habits

A habit is a habit, so you might as well have good ones. What are you committed to doing regularly? Who are the people you spend time with? When do you have opportunity to read God's Word and pray during the week? Who can you study the Bible and worship with? Having a pattern to our lives, with some regular commitments, can have a positive effect. If we just follow our feelings when deciding how to spend our time, we will sometimes, when we are at our most tired and vulnerable, put ourselves in the way of maximum temptation and opportunity. Our patterns of sleeping, eating and exercise are also relevant here. Learning to control our bodies in one area of life is much easier if we are also controlling them in other areas. If we behave stupidly and self-indulgently in some areas, it is extremely unlikely that we will be godly in our sexuality.

A habit I am often asked about is masturbation – stimulating yourself sexually. The Bible does not talk about it directly, but there are some problems with it nevertheless. It can become compulsive; it can distort our view of other people, and it can develop fantasy and lust in our minds. It is not the unforgivable sin, and adolescent exploratory masturbation may involve different issues from masturbating as a long-term coping mechanism. But masturbation can certainly make us more self-centred, and definitely lacks any clear emotional context. If we carry on doing something that we believe to be wrong, then we damage ourselves and undermine confidence in our relationship with God.

Woody Allen said, 'Don't knock masturbation, it's sex with someone I love.' I do not believe that masturbation is an expression of love, and certainly few people feel more loved after the experience. It is possible to see change and growth in this area. Masturbation does little to alleviate loneliness. It is a short-term solution to long-term problems.

develop honest, supportive relationships

God does not want us to live the Christian life on our own. It is vitally important to have good friends whom we respect as Christians and get on well with, and with whom we can be open and honest. This is an important aspect of getting right with God and of beginning to move some of our struggles from the private to the public arena.

Talking problems through helps to own them, understand them and confront them.

When Paul describes the 'armour of God' in Ephesians 6, he mentions 'the shield of faith'. The Roman soldier's shield, which he had in mind, was large. It was at its most effective when deployed with other shields. A soldier could not protect his side or back with his own shield, but standing together with others afforded good protection. When we are open and accountable to each other, we are standing together and protecting each other's vulnerable points.

a case study: David

We may be able to understand some of these principles better by looking at the account of David and Bathsheba in 2 Samuel 11. We can trace seven steps in David's descent into sexual sin.

1. David forgot who he was (verse 1)

He was the king. It was the time of year when kings went to war. David should have been at war with the army, but instead, he was back in Jerusalem. Past exploits of heroism were no excuse for this dereliction of duty. He should have been doing what was appropriate to his calling; he should have been in the battle because of the position to which God had appointed him. But David had disregarded his responsibilities and gone his own way. His attempt to withdraw from the conflict and choose a life of ease was to have profound consequences for himself and the people of God.

2. David was in the wrong place (verse 2a)

Instead of being at camp, focused on the battle, David went for a stroll on the roof of his palace. Having stepped aside from God's plan for his life, he was now in jeopardy. Had he been in the right place, the temptation he was about to face would never have arisen. What we see here is a misuse of position. David's sensitivity and responsibility set him above question, and this makes him vulnerable to temptation.

3. David looked with lust (verse 2b)

From his vantage-point he could not help seeing the beautiful Bathsheba taking a bath. The first look is not lustful. It is in the second that the lust begins. Our eyes see many images and scenes that arouse our appetites and desires; the danger lies in taking a second look. David was now looking, and as he looked his desire grew. The simple act of looking effects a change of heart. David has not been keeping God's law in his heart and is now vulnerable to the lust of his eyes. Disregarding God's law in one area of our lives has repercussions in others.

4. David made an inappropriate investigation (verse 3a)

He enquired about Bathsheba. He had no business finding out about her; he was married. He discovered that she was married. There are some things it is better not to find out about. When lust leads on to investigations, we begin to translate desires into possibilities, and possibilities into opportunities. This happens gradually, and it is easy to close our minds to what is going on.

We can only speculate at David's thought processes at this point. The usual pattern is to move from denial ('Nothing will happen') to rationalization ('I can handle it', or 'I deserve this'), to self-justification ('It's not that bad under the circumstances') to transfer of responsibility ('The other person will stop if it's wrong'). Lack of resolve at this stage is critical. When integrity goes, ambiguity is the first thing to take its place. Losing the battle in the mind opens the door to the possibility of capitulating in our actions.

5. David disregarded the truth (verses 3b–5)

He had Bathsheba brought to the palace. This was a misuse of his position and of the gifts God had given him. He disobeyed God's law and disregarded the promises he made. He slept with Bathsheba – not an act of passion, swept away in the heat of the moment, but a premeditated and deliberate act. Sexual sin tends to be like this. In the heat of the moment, often we simply carry through to its logical conclusion a plan we have made already. David could not argue that he could not help himself. He had made a succession of poor decisions which had led him to this point. Now Bathsheba was pregnant.

6. David tried to cover up (verses 6–17)

He had Uriah summoned back from the battle-front in an attempt to cover up his sin. If he could just get Uriah to sleep with Bathsheba, he would think the baby was his own. We often hope that we can cover up our wrongdoings before they become known, and pretend that it was the responsibility of somebody else. Uriah, in his response, demonstrated himself to be a man of integrity. Greater commitment to God's cause was modelled by this man, who was not even a Jew, than by God's anointed king. David was not moved by this example, and hardened his heart. When his tactics failed, he devised an even more heinous scheme; he engineered Uriah's death in battle.

7. David thought he had got away with it (verses 26–27)

After a period of mourning for her husband, Bathsheba was taken to live in the palace. She became David's wife and the child was born within that union. For the moment it looked as though David's sin would not become known. But the Lord knew, and we read, 'The thing David had done displeased the LORD.' It seems too that Israel's enemies, the Ammonites, at whose hand Uriah had fallen, knew what had gone on; they showed 'utter contempt' (12:14). God's people and name were disgraced because of David's action. David did *not* get away with it. The prophet Nathan came and rebuked him. David repented in great sorrow, but the child died (see chapter 12).

It is worth taking time to consider your own situation and to go through the steps in David's downward career, identifying where he went wrong and asking where you might be going wrong. There may well be changes you need to make. If nothing else, we should learn from David how a little bit of 'harmless' self-indulgence can lead to more serious actions, which have far-reaching consequences.

It is salutary to see how someone like David could get into this position. It helps me to remember that there is nothing that I am not capable of, given the opportunity. It is too easy to point the finger at others and to be judgmental. People who fail and fall need compassion, support and help. David's private failure became a public scandal. It is a story that should both move us and sharpen our senses to danger. I find remembering the steps in David's failure very useful in dealing with temptation in my own life.

15. forgiveness

Failure is not fatal. Forgiveness is for ever.

Many of us suffer from the scars of messed-up relationships, which are still sore. In the immediate aftermath of a relationship, a situation that has gone wrong, or a mistake that has been made, the hurt can be very acute. These events can entail consequences and leave memories which stay with us for a long time. Yet no matter how serious these failures feel, they are not fatal.

> Because of the LORD's great love we are not consumed,
>   for his compassions never fail.
> They are new every morning;
>   great is your faithfulness.
>
> (Lamentations 3:22)

God's commitment to us is not deflected by our disobedience. He does not treat us as we deserve, but delights to take the initiative in drawing close to us. Often it is in the darkest moments that we meet him and discover that he can bring healing, wholeness and forgiveness to our broken hearts. He is in the business of mending broken lives. The forgiveness that Jesus offers is the only meaningful orgiveness.

God does not dismiss our sin or treat it lightly. Forgiveness does not mean saying, 'There, there, it doesn't matter.' We must be alert to the danger of justifying and excusing our behaviour. It is perfectly possible to deny that we have done anything wrong and yet to be guilty of sexual wrongdoing. This denial of reality may lead to a cycle of activity or escapism where the very behaviour that has caused the sexual guilt is repeated to avoid facing up to it. This can be true of patterns of behaviour in relationships, or of habits like the use of pornography. It is not possible for us to escape from our sin or to blot it out by our own activities or efforts. We must be willing to face our wrong behaviour and attitudes and acknowledge them for what they are. Rebellion against God matters wherever and whenever it takes place. To pretend otherwise is to devalue Christ's death on the cross.

The cross is a constant reminder that sin is serious and has profound consequences. God was willing to face the fact of our sinfulness. His forgiveness was not cheap, but was bought for us at great price. Calvary is the supreme demonstration of God's love for us. Jesus took the punishment we deserved. The resurrection proves that God accepted his sacrifice once and for all. He removes our sin as far away from us as the East is from the West (Psalm 103:12). His forgiveness is free and for ever.

This cleansing and total forgiveness were experienced by David after his adultery with Bathsheba. When God sent the prophet Nathan to challenge him, David realized that what he had done was wrong. His response of repentance and receiving God's forgiveness is recorded in Psalm 51.

> Have mercy on me, O God,
>   according to your unfailing love;
> According to your great compassion
>   blot out my transgressions.
> Wash away all my iniquity
>   and cleanse me from my sin.

> For I know my transgressions,
>   and my sin is always before me.
> Against you, you only, have I sinned
>   and done what is evil in your sight.

David recognized that he had sinned against God. This perspective is very important. When we do wrong, it is not just a case of damaging ourselves or upsetting other people, but of hurting God. The consequences of our actions may be profound on a human level, but this should not blind us to the even more serious underlying spiritual reality. Sin is ultimately sin against God and an offence to his character. It is worth reading through the rest of Psalm 51 yourself, as it offers many valuable insights into repentance and forgiveness. You may also find these words from Ezekiel helpful in thinking about the work of God in the life of his people:

> I will sprinkle clean water on you, and you will be clean; I will cleanse you from all your impurities and from all your idols. I will give you a new heart and put a new spirit in you; I will remove from you your heart of stone and give you a heart of flesh. And I will put my Spirit in you and move you to follow my decrees and be careful to keep my laws. (Ezekiel 36:25–27)

God has promised to forgive us when we ask. A clean heart for a new start is not just possible; it can be actual. There is no sin or wrongdoing that is beyond God's forgiveness. Jesus died for sexual sin as well as all the rest.

important steps to forgiveness

do not harden your heart

Truth demands a response. When God challenges us with truth about himself, our character, our relationships, habits, desires, plans and activities, we are faced with a choice. We can either listen to

God or harden our hearts. Both of these are responses to the truth, but one leads to life and hope, and the other to death and destruction. Part of God's work in our lives is to give us living hearts which beat with his heartbeat. Every time we harden our hearts, we push God away from the centre of our being.

repent

Repentance is not something we have to do in order to come back to God. It is the act of coming back to God itself. Repentance means a change of mind, a reversal in direction, a turning away from ourselves and a turning back to God. Most of us are sorry for our actions from time to time and experience genuine regret, but this is not repentance. Paul distinguishes between this kind of sorrow and what he calls 'Godly sorrow': 'Godly sorrow brings repentance that leads to salvation and leaves no regret, but worldly sorrow brings death' (2 Corinthians 7:10).

The difference between Godly sorrow and feeling sorry for ourselves is that the first produces change, whereas the second leaves us where we were. Godly sorrow comes from God. We become convinced that we have done wrong. This may happen through our consciences, through circumstances or through deep conviction. God can use all these to bring us to our senses. This is a key part of the work of the Holy Spirit in us. The effects of godly sorrow are a change of mind and direction, which leads to forgiveness. Turning back to God has immediate benefits and also brings the possibility of being left with no regret.

Worldly sorrow leaves us continuing in the same direction to repeat our mistakes in the future. Too often, people experience worldly sorrow, regretting the consequences of their actions, but refuse to admit that what they have done is an offence against God. Because wrongdoing is behaviour contrary to God's character, all sin is ultimately against God. As such, it can be forgiven only by him. There may well be consequences to work through and issues to be resolved with other people, but only God can forgive us.

God did what we could not do ourselves, and paid the penalty for our sin. He has promised that 'if we confess our sins, he is faithful and just and will forgive us our sins and purify us from all unrighteousness' (John 1:9). This promise of unconditional forgiveness and total cleansing is a precious gift.

Lift your weary head, my child,
And fly away with me
To a place of which you've dreamed before
But never thought you'd see
Where the past is all forgiven
And innocence is free.

Lift your head, my child,
And fly away with me.
You've grown so old so quickly
Living only for today.
Virginity, serenity
You've lost along the way.
But forgotten childhood treasures
And sweet abandoned dreams
Wait in joy for you;
Come fly away with me.

All the time you've wasted
On yourself has tied you down,
But my love has cut those ropes
To set you free.
The bitter tears you've tasted
Will be diamonds in your crown.
So rejoice, my child,
And fly away with me.

I know that you don't understand
How life beings again,
But trust me now

> Don't be afraid;
> I've paid for all your sin.
> The life that I've poured out for you
> Has restored your purity
> Lift your head, my child,
> And fly away with me.
>
> (From 'Growing Pains' by Jamie Owens)

It is often at our lowest points that the grace of God comes most clearly to us. It is when we feel the least lovely that we can most appreciate unconditional love. The love that we experience with other people can be cruel and fragile and leave us hurting. The love that God shows to us is true, lasting and healing. God loves to draw close to us in our pain and weakness. He is able to fix the biggest mess and to begin to transform lives and situations by his divine power.

Getting right with God is the key, but it is not the end of the story. Redemption is a process that looks towards the future. Altered attitudes will follow repentance and renewal. The greatest adventure in life is the challenge of true Christian commitment. This may well involve tough, costly decisions. Even if our personal happiness in the short term has to diminish, this could be for the best. We may need to begin to handle our emotional lives much more thoughtfully and be prepared to delay the gratification of our desires. We shall certainly need to seek help from those around us.

pray

Take time to include the following elements as you pray:

— *Thank you*
  Thank God for your life ... God's grace ... your friends ... God's love and character ... his desire to draw close to you, to speak to you and to listen ... the death of his Son on the cross ... the Holy Spirit who helps you.

— *Sorry*

Confess your sins to God. Take time to name and talk through all that you have done that has hurt him and affected other people.

— *Please*

Ask for God's forgiveness, remembering what he has promised. Ask the Holy Spirit to help you live differently. Ask for grace and courage as you recommit yourself to living God's way.

commit yourself to living differently

Getting right with God means committing yourself to change. You may well need to put matters right with other people. It is important to talk through with an older Christian the response you have made. Take time to discuss its implications. Trying to sort something out on your own may serve only to compound the damage. Many of these issues can be properly dealt with only within the context of the church family. This is one more reason why church membership and commitment to a fellowship are so vitally important for authentic Christian life.

You may find it helpful to write down the commitments you are making to God. This may serve as a useful reminder in the future.

We will continue to make mistakes and get things wrong. Our need of God's grace will not diminish as we get older. We must never settle for mediocrity or compromise, but persevere in our calling to work out our salvation with fear and trembling – knowing it is God who works in us to will and to act according to his good purpose (Philippians 2:12–13). The Holy Spirit has been sent to help us. One of his key jobs is to guide us towards holiness. We will find that God will pinpoint specific behaviours or attitudes or relationships that are wrong and need to change. This is proof of his ongoing commitment to us and reminds us that we are his children. Note that God's challenges will be specific. This is a key way to distinguish God's voice from the blanket condemnation with which the devil tries to smother us. God tells us in his Word that there is no condemnation for those who are in Christ Jesus (Romans 8:1). God is for us, not against us, and he is able to bring help, healing and wholeness into the most broken and hopeless situation.

My conscience was hardened by widely conflicting ideas taught by Christian leaders about what was and was not acceptable before marriage. I used to think of God as a spoilsport, but now I think his plan is the best idea. I wish someone had told me sooner. (James, 26)

God is loving and forgiving. We need to accept his grace. Short-term snogging sessions, and even longer, steady relationships (unless they are what God has planned for us) do not bring us closer to God. It is difficult to know what is right when the most important subject of today is not being hammered in church. Only recently have I grasped the fact that, because I have repented of the many shameful things I have done, God has forgiven me. I am now determined to live in obedience to God. (Sandy, 19)

I've struggled with masturbation since I was 11 years old. Whenever I tried to stop, it never worked. It became addictive. Then, after hearing a talk on sexuality, I confessed it to God. I haven't struggled with it since. That was eighteen months ago. He can do the impossible. (Phil, 22)

Many of these ideas will become reality only as we grow in our understanding of what it means to be the church. A wholehearted commitment to mutual growth can flourish only in the church environment. The church is not something Christians go to; it is something we belong to. We come together to celebrate and experience a oneness with each other and with God which is a foretaste of a greater communion to come. The church is not yet all it will be, nor all it can be. But it is the context God has created for our spiritual lives.

God has not finished with us yet. The church is still being built. He challenges us to participate in this building programme. Every act of trust, every expression of faith, and every decision to love helps to build the church. The risk that we take in being vulnerable before imperfect people like ourselves is one of the ways we express our Christian commitment. God's love is made complete when we love each other.

We cannot communicate the reality of God's forgiveness to others unless we can forgive each other. We cannot experience the fullness of God's forgiveness while we withhold it from others.

Forgiveness is best ministered from a position of vulnerability. When others speak to us about their sins and failures, we must fight any temptation to think of ourselves as superior. We should respond compassionately, as we would want them to respond to us. Here are some tips.

Listen. Let people talk, and pay attention to what they say. Ask questions that enable them to open up, not 'yes/no' questions or ones that hint at how you think they should feel: 'How do you feel about that?' rather than 'Do you feel guilty about that?' But avoid unhelpful details. You do not need to know everything, and should not ask.

Accept other people as God accepts you. Sometimes it is hard not to show that you are shocked by a disclosure or confession. Remember we are all sinners. There are worse things about ourselves that we don't know yet, but God knows, and still accepts us. Part of our accepting others may mean receiving their anger, frustration or pain without retaliating or condemning.

Forgive. This does not mean telling them, 'Everyone does that, so it doesn't matter.' Don't cheapen grace. Remind them of the central truths of the gospel. Remember God's grace, and his promise that, if we confess our sins, he is faithful and just and will forgive and purify us (1 John 1:9). We can help to communicate this forgiveness to others. The forgiveness we minister and affirm is not given on our own authority, but comes through faith in Christ, who died and rose again to pay the penalty for our sin.

Encourage. Bringing difficult issues into the open before God is painful, but positive. It is a sign of grace and growth. We are often keen to say that we have learned our lesson, and to draw a line under sin. God is concerned to deal not only with our sin, but with its causes. Its roots run deep, but God's forgiveness is complete and his commitment to us continues. He draws the line through the sin and, our learning goes on. When we talk about what God is teaching us, we should be careful to use the continuous tense: 'I am beginning to learn ...' I am still learning lessons that I started to learn years ago. Whenever I am tempted to say I have finally learned something, I am almost certain to have missed the point! We need to encourage each other to keep learning and to grow in grace. There may well be definite changes we need to make, consequences to work through, positive relationships to encourage and practical steps to commit to.

Refer. It is important to recognize when you are out of your depth and need to refer your friend to someone else. This may be an older Christian in your church, a minister, pastor or elder, or a professional counsellor. (A list of agencies is given in the 'Resources' appendix.) It is entirely normal to need this kind of extra support for a while. It is not always easy to find the right person, but we should not be tempted to fill this vacuum ourselves. Untold damage can be caused by attempting to help people beyond our capacity to do so effectively.

We shall need realism and determination to keep going. Change will not be easy, nor will it happen overnight. Our progress is marked not so much by how often we fall, but by how often we allow God to help us back up again. Daily repentance and continual asking for God's forgiveness must be the pattern of our lives. The longer we persevere, the more we shall realize our need of God's grace. He has promised to carry through to completion the work he has started in us. We must keep going. Those who plod on will be applauded, but it is those who finish who win the prize (see Philippians 3:13–14; Hebrews 12:1). We experience a foretaste of what is to come, but the perfection, intimacy and rescue that we long for will not be ours until Christ returns.

Until then, let us commit ourselves to living with integrity; playing our part in Christian communities; giving ourselves daily in Christ's service; and being the best that we can be – living radical, revolutionary lives.

resources

resources

The Relationships Revolution e-mail: RelRev@uccf.org.uk

CARE
53 Romney Street
London SW1P 3RF
Tel. 0171 233 0455
Co-ordinating body for practical caring initiatives nationwide. Has a network of trained counsellors across the country.

CARE for the family
PO Box 488
Cardiff CF1 1RE
Tel. 01222 811733
For further help and advice for staff or church helpers. (Contact Anne Carlos)

homosexuality

True Freedom Trust
PO Box 3
Upton
Wirral
Merseyside L49 6NY
Tel. 0151 653 0773
E-mail martin@tftrust.u-net.com
Internet www.tftrust.u-net.com
Teaching and counselling ministry. (Contact Martin Hallett)

pregnancy advice

CARE for life
PO Box 389
Basingstoke RG24 9QF
Tel. 01256 477300
A department of CARE. Supports local caring initiatives providing practical alternatives to (or care after) abortion. Centres and contacts across England and Scotland.

HIV/AIDS

ACET (Aids Care Education and Training)
PO Box 1323
London W5 5TF
Advice and practical caring ministry for those with HIV/AIDS.

bereavement

Cruse
126 Sheen Road
Richmond
Surrey TW9 1UR
Tel. 0181 940 4818
Cruse youthline 0181 940 3131
Network of counsellors dealing specifically with bereavement counselling.

eating disorders

Anorexia and Bulimia Care
15 Fernhurst Gate
Aughton
Lancashire L39 5ED
Tel. 01695 422479
E-mail Doreenabc@compuserve.com